Representation

Key Concepts in Political Science

GENERAL EDITOR: Leonard Schapiro
EXECUTIVE EDITOR: Peter Calvert

Other titles in the same series include:

ALREADY PUBLISHED

IN PREPARATION

Representation

A. H. Birch

University of Exeter

Pall Mall · London

Pall Mall Press Limited
5 Cromwell Place, London sw7

First published 1971
© 1971 by Pall Mall Press Limited
ISBN 0 269 02694 0

Set by Gloucester Typesetting Co. Ltd
Gloucester

Printed in Great Britain at
the Pitman Press, Bath

Contents

'Key Concepts'
an Introductory Note

Political concepts are part of our daily speech—we abuse 'bureaucracy' and praise 'democracy', welcome or recoil from 'revolution'. Emotive words such as 'equality', 'dictatorship', 'élite' or even 'power' can often, by the very passions which they raise, obscure a proper understanding of the sense in which they are, or should be, or should not be, or have been used. Confucius regarded the 'rectification of names' as the first task of government. 'If names are not correct, language will not be in accordance with the truth of things', and this in time would lead to the end of justice, to anarchy and to war. One could with some truth point out that the attempts hitherto by governments to enforce their own quaint meanings on words have not been conspicuous for their success in the advancement of justice. 'Rectification of names' there must certainly be: but most of us would prefer such rectification to take place in the free debate of the university, in the competitive arena of the pages of the book or journal.

Analysis of commonly used political terms, their reassessment or their 'rectification', is, of course, normal activity in the political science departments of our universities. The idea of this series was indeed born in the course of discussion between a few university teachers of political science, of whom Professor S. E. Finer of Manchester University was one. It occurred to us that a series of short books discussing the 'Key Concepts' in political science would serve two purposes. In universities these books could provide the kind of brief political texts which might be of assistance to students in gaining a fuller understanding of the terms which they were constantly using. But we also hoped that outside the universities there exists a reading public which has the time, the curiosity and the inclination to pause to reflect on some of those words and ideas which are so often taken for granted. Perhaps even 'that insidious and crafty animal', as Adam Smith described the politician and statesman, will occasionally derive some pleasure or even profit from that more leisurely analysis which academic study can afford, and which a busy life in the practice of politics often denies.

It has been very far from the minds of those who have been concerned in planning and bringing into being the 'Key Concepts' series to try and impose (as if that were possible!) any uniform pattern on the authors who have contributed, or will contribute, to it. I, for one, hope that each author will, in his own individual manner, seek and find the best way of helping us to a fuller understanding of the concept which he has chosen to analyse. But whatever form the individual exposition may take, there are, I believe, three aspects of illumination which we can confidently expect from each volume in this series. First, we can look for some examination of the history of the concept, and of its evolution against a changing social and political background. I believe, as many do who are concerned with the study of political science, that it is primarily in history that the explanation must be sought for many of the perplexing problems of political analysis and judgement which beset us today. Second, there is the semantic aspect. To look in depth at a 'key concept' necessarily entails a study of the name which attached itself to it; of the different ways in which, and the different purposes for which, the name was used; of the way in which in the course of history the same name was applied to several concepts, or several names were applied to one and the same concept; and, indeed, of the changes which the same concept, or what appears to be the same concept, has undergone in the course of time. This analysis will usually require a searching examination of the relevant literature in order to assess the present stage of scholarship in each particular field. And thirdly, I hope that the reader of each volume in this series will be able to decide for himself what the proper and valid use should be of a familiar term in politics, and will gain, as it were, from each volume a sharper and better-tempered tool of political analysis.

There are many today who would disagree with Bismarck's view that politics can never be an exact science. I express no opinion on this much debated question. But all of us who are students of politics—and our numbers both inside and outside the universities continue to grow—will be the better for knowing what precisely we mean when we use a common political term.

<table>
<tr><td>London School of Economics
and Political Science</td><td>Leonard Schapiro
General Editor</td></tr>
</table>

To J. P. Lees

Acknowledgements

I should like to thank Dr Robert Dowse, Professor Maurice Goldsmith and Dr Noel O'Sullivan, each of whom has been generous with criticisms and advice. I am also grateful to my wife for her constant support and assistance and to Miss Elizabeth Brown for typing an untidy manuscript in a cheerful and highly efficient manner. I made the mistakes myself.

I have dedicated the book to my former tutor at Nottingham, who laboured not only in tutorials but also over innumerable pints of beer to develop my interest in political theory, and to whom I shall always be grateful for the stimulation and encouragement he gave me.

Exeter 1971   A.H.B.

1/The Meaning of Representation

The concept of representation is a familiar concept of everyday life which is used not only in both political and non-political situations but also in a variety of ways. When people speak of a representative sample they are not using the term 'representative' in quite the same way as they are when they speak of a sales representative or a legal representative. When they talk of an elected representative or a system of representative government the connotations of the term are different again. There may be some common element in these usages, but any exploration of the concept of representation must start by acknowledging that the concept is far from simple.

In this type of situation the traditional approach of philosophers, from the Greeks onwards, has been to search for the essential meaning of the concept under consideration. Plato's *Republic* was an attempt to uncover the essential meaning of the concept of justice, while subsequent philosophers have tried to penetrate to the heart of such concepts as authority, liberty, and equality. In the present century, philosophers in England (and subsequently elsewhere) have tended to reject this approach as unhelpful. Words have usages, it is said, rather than essential meanings, and a careful analysis of their various usages is likely to be more fruitful than a concentration of attention on the common element in these usages, which may be of only etymological significance.

The only thorough study that has so far been made of the concept of representation, that by Hanna F. Pitkin,[1] while somewhat influenced by this approach, nevertheless clings to the older idea that the object of the analysis is to discover the 'real nature' of the concept. Hanna Pitkin's examination of the various theories of representation that have been advanced in the past three centuries is intended to build up a picture of the thing itself, much as one may discover the nature of a complex structure by examining flash bulb photographs of it taken from various angles.[2] Each photograph gives a partial and misleading picture of the thing—she would say a wrong picture[3]—but by comparing them the careful student can piece together a reasonable understanding of what the structure is really like.

It implies no disrespect to a valuable piece of scholarship to say that this approach makes the whole problem seem a great deal more difficult than it need be. The problem becomes much easier if one starts with the approach recommended by Wittgenstein, who likened the relationship between usages of a term to the resemblance between members of a family. If one wishes to understand a family one must study the character of its members: their similarities will emerge but their differences are equally important, and it would be foolish to try to portray them all as manifestations of a single essential family character. If the student of political representation begins with this kind of approach it can be seen that his first task is to understand the character of the established usages of the term, without making the assumption that these can all be reduced to a single definition. He need not go to the other extreme and adopt the role of a lexicographer, charting all the vagaries of common speech. He must drop the assumption of a single meaning, but careful analysis of the usages of the term will lead to the identification of a limited number of main usages, each logically distinct from the others. This can then serve as the basis for further analysis of the concept, it being accepted that in common speech people often slip thoughtlessly from one usage to another and blur the distinctions between them.

The second task of the student is to understand the nature of the main argument about the various types of representation that have been advanced by political theorists in different historical periods. His third task is to appreciate the ways in which these arguments have influenced, and are reflected in, contemporary political behaviour and his fourth task is to assess the value of various concepts of representation in empirical studies of politics. If he does all this he will understand the concept of representation, and there is no need at all for him to try to reduce the various usages and theories to a single definition, any more than he need pronounce some of them to be correct and others incorrect.

The main usages of the term 'representative'

There are three main ways in which the term 'represent-ative' is commonly used, together with various specialized or subsidiary usages. The three main usages, each logically distinct from the others, are as follows:

1   to denote an agent or spokesman who acts on behalf of his principal
2   to indicate that a person shares some of the character-istics of a class of persons
3   to indicate that a person symbolizes the identity or qualities of a class of persons.

In the first of these usages, the term designates a person who has the acknowledged duty of defending or advancing certain interests specified by his principal. A sales representative is a representative in this sense of the term; so is a man sent by a duellist to arrange the location and weapons of the duel with his opponent's representative; so is an ambassador; and so is a lawyer appointed to defend the interests of his client in a court hearing. The representative does not necessarily act exactly as his principal would; in some situations the representative may drive a harder bargain than his principal would feel able to do, while in others the representative may be restrained by professional etiquette and conventions. But in all cases the function of this kind of representative is to achieve certain goals set by his principal, and the extent to which these goals are achieved is a criterion of successful representation. As a form of shorthand, this kind of representation will henceforth be described as delegated representation.

One question which commonly arises in connection with dele-gated representation is the extent to which the representative is, or should be, bound by the instructions of his principal. This ques-tion has been discussed in scores of books, hundreds of articles, thousands of speeches. No agreement has been reached on the answer, for the simple reason that no meaningful answer is possible when the question is phrased in general terms. It is a question to which the answer depends almost entirely on the exact circum-stances of the representative relationship under discussion. For example, a lawyer cannot be so closely bound by his client's in-structions as a sales representative can be bound by his firm's instructions, because the lawyer is governed by a strict code of professional behaviour and has duties to the court as well as to his client. How closely the lawyer will follow instructions also depends on the nature of the case: a lawyer in a divorce case might expect to receive fairly detailed instructions about the kind of evidence to call and the kind of settlement to work for, whereas a lawyer defending a man charged with murder would expect a fairly free hand in reaching decisions about the best line of defence.

Another question which often arises is the extent to which a representative of this kind can bind his principal. It is sometimes assumed that if such a representative agrees to a proposal this can be taken to imply the consent of the principal. In fact this is only sometimes the case. The relationship between representation and consent varies, and depends on all sorts of contingent factors. Thus modern ambassadors hardly ever have power to commit their governments, but when international communications were slower ambassadors were sometimes given such powers. The relationship between representation and commitment or consent is therefore (like the question of instructions) a matter for historical enquiry, depending as it does on the exact circumstances of each situation.

The statement that a man is a representative in the sense of being an agent conveys only a limited amount of information. It does not tell us how the man was appointed, what kind of man he is, whether he acts under close or loose instructions, or whether his agreement to a proposal binds his principal. However, it does tell us something about his functions and probable behaviour, and is therefore to be sharply distinguished from the second general usage of the term, which refers not to the functions but to the descriptive characteristics of the representative.

This second usage is well exemplified in the term 'representative sample', which indicates a sample of the relevant population chosen by statistical methods so that the main characteristics of the population will be mirrored in the sample. The term is used in the same sense, but more loosely, to denote a person who is in some respects typical of a larger class of persons to which he belongs. This usage occurs in such statements as 'the varied membership of the club is represented fairly well in the composition of the executive committee' or 'a state assembly full of lawyers is hardly representative of the farmers whose produce is the basis of the state's prosperity'.

Since a representative body would be ideally constituted, in this sense of the term, if it were a microcosm of the larger society, this kind of representation will henceforth be described as microcosmic representation.

The statement that a man is a representative in this sense does not tell us anything about his functions or intentions or even about his behaviour. It simply tells us something about his personal characteristics. Sometimes there is a degree of confusion about this. Thus, if a professor of international relations were conducting a seminar on Middle Eastern problems in an American university he might call upon an Arab student to expound the Arab viewpoint and introduce him as 'a representative of the Arab world'. In fact this student's views might not be typical of Arab views and he might not be able to put up such a good defence of the politics of Arab states as an American student could. As a spokesman for the Arab world he might be a complete failure. But a special significance would probably be attached to his contribution because of his nationality, and subsequent speakers might weigh their words more carefully than they would if no 'representative of the Arab world' were present.

The third main usage is found when someone is described as representing a number of persons in a symbolic way. The term 'symbol' is normally applied to an emblem or physical object which calls to mind some larger and usually more abstract entity. Thus, the hammer and sickle is a symbol of the u.s.s.r.; the Christian cross is a symbol of the crucifixion; and the scales of justice symbolize the essential character of the law. In a similar fashion a symbolic representative calls to mind, or serves as a concrete embodiment of, a whole group or category of persons. In Christian theology Adam was the symbolic representative of all mankind when he fell from grace and Jesus Christ filled the same role when he died on the cross to redeem our sins. In Marx's writings the proletariat is depicted as the symbolic representative of all humanity, having 'a universal character because its sufferings are universal' and not claiming 'a particular redress because the wrong which is done to it is not a particular wrong but wrong in general'.[4] On a more limited scale, the Unknown Warrior whose bones lie in Westminster Abbey is a symbolic representative of all British soldiers who perished in the two World Wars.

This usage is neither as common nor as important as the other two kinds of usage, but it must not be ignored because symbolic representation—and the demand for symbolic representation—plays a significant part in political activity.

Political representation

A political representative is a person who, by custom or law, has the status or role of a representative within a political system. The definition of this latter term is unfortunately not so easy, as the exact meaning of the term 'political' is open to question.

One obvious starting point is to say that political activity is essentially communication with a purpose, that purpose being to arrive at a collective decision or to resolve a dispute. But this is insufficiently precise, as it could include discussions in a university seminar or argument about which football team has the best record. It can be made more precise by saying that the purpose of political activity is to influence or determine the decisions of those who wield authority in society, thus linking politics firmly with the process of civil government. This is the line taken by David Easton, who has defined the object of politics as 'the authoritative allocation of values in a society'.[5] But while this approach is logical and convenient, it has two distinct limitations. On the one hand, it excludes activities which are commonly regarded as political even though they take place within private associations, such as disputes over policy within a trade union. On the other hand, it seems to exclude the realm of international politics, where nobody exercises authority.

While it is thus difficult to regard this as an entirely satisfactory way of defining politics, it is also difficult to improve upon it. It seems impossible to produce a short definition of political activity that is narrow enough to exclude activities that are more properly described as economic or social or military or academic, but broad enough to include such varied phenomena as the selection of trade-union leaders, the resolution of disputes in a nomadic tribe, the government of a modern industrial state, diplomatic relations between states, and the activities of the Vietcong or the Palestine Liberation Front. We must therefore content ourselves with a rough and approximate characterization of political activity, such as that it is the activity of governing a community or association, together with those activities which are designed to influence the decisions that are taken during the process of government. Widely interpreted, this could include the attempts by one government to influence the politics of another, and could thus include international politics as well as the politics of the nation state and of local authorities and associations within the state.

A political system can be defined simply as a set of political activities which are functionally related to one another and have some continuity in time. Political representatives have a variety of roles within such a system. They may be delegated representatives, such as the British representative on the Security Council, the American representative at the Vietnam peace talks which opened in Paris in 1968, or the spokesmen for pressure groups who play a prominent part in the legislative process in most advanced countries. They may be representatives in the microcosmic sense, as illustrated by the determination of the Labour Representative Committee to secure the election of working men to Parliament or by the conventions which determine that each Canadian cabinet shall contain so many French Canadians, so many members from Ontario, and so many members from the western provinces. They may be representatives in the symbolic sense, as monarchs or presidents are often regarded as the symbolic representative of the nation as a whole.

However, most of the controversies over political representation have revolved around the choice and functions of elected members of a representative assembly, whose position cannot be equated easily with any of the three main types of representation defined above. To some extent, at least, they generally act as spokesmen for their electors, but the nature of the proper relationship between elected persons and their constituents has been a matter of dispute for several centuries and it would certainly be wrong to regard elected representatives as being essentially agents for those who elected them. That they should act in this way is a common recommendation, but it follows from this that they do not necessarily act in this way and therefore cannot be defined in these terms.

In fact, the description of elected members of a political assembly as representatives is best regarded as a specialized usage of the term, not exactly equivalent to any non-political usage. The essential characteristic of such persons is the manner of their selection, not their behaviour or characteristics or symbolic value. Of course, the concept of election is occasionally the subject of controversy, since some writers define it in a purely formal and procedural way whereas others claim that it implies freedom of choice, with all that this involves. Since acceptance of this claim would mean that the members of most of the world's political assemblies could not be described as elected representatives, it will be convenient in this context to think of election as a formal procedure, not necessarily implying competition or freedom.[6]

Are elected representatives also representatives in any or all of the three general usages of the term? The answer to this is that they may or may not be, although it is constantly urged by interested parties that they ought to be. Innumerable writers and speakers have maintained that elected representatives have a duty to act as agents for their constituents, and in some countries at some periods this has been the prevailing view. On the other hand, the most influential theorists in the Western world have stressed the need for elected representatives to do whatever they think best for the nation as a whole while other writers again have insisted that the first duty of an elected person is to support his party. The significance and validity of instructions and mandates has been a recurrent theme in the perennial debate about political representation.

Another recurrent theme in this debate is the view that, ideally, elected representatives should be similar to their electors, so that the assembly would be a social microcosm of the nation. Advocates of this view have suggested that an assembly cannot be properly representative of the nation if its social composition is conspicuously different from that of the electorate. In homogeneous societies such as Britain this kind of argument, though often used as a basis for criticizing existing institutions, has rarely cut much ice, but in societies divided on social or religious lines its impact has naturally been much greater. Ethnic loyalties in American cities have led to the practice whereby the parties nominate a 'balanced ticket' for election, each party's list of candidates containing a suitable proportion of Irish-Americans, Italian-Americans and so on. In African and Asian states issues of this kind are much more critical: it should always be remembered that a crucial step in the developments which led up to the partition of India was that taken when

Jinnah, the leader of the Muslim League, insisted that as the Muslim League represented all Muslims and the Congress Party was (in his view) a Hindu party, he could no longer accept Muslims nominated by the Congress Party as legitimate representatives of anybody.[7]

It follows that both the first and second general usages of the term 'representative' have been prominent in the debates about elected representatives. Symbolic representation has been much less prominent, as it has rarely been canvassed openly. But there can be no doubt that in many political situations the election or appointment of a representative of a minority group has a significance out of all proportion to the real power he enjoys because he symbolizes the recognition of the political rights of the group in question. Obvious examples are the nomination and Senate confirmation of Thurgood Marshall as the first black member of the U.S. Supreme Court, the election of black politicians as mayors in Cleveland and Newark, and the appointment of Sir Learie Constantine (a West Indian) to the House of Lords in 1968.

Elected representatives may therefore be representatives in any or none of the three main senses outlined earlier in this chapter. The nature of political representation is a complex matter which cannot be understood by formulating a definition, but only by examining the debates about representation that have taken place in various historical situations. It is for this reason that in the next chapters we shall look back into the past.

2/Medieval Concepts and Practices

To understand the nature of modern concepts of political representation, some account must be given of the historical developments which led to the emergence of these concepts. Most modern debates on the subject are conducted in terms of ideas which were first advanced many decades (if not centuries) ago and the only way to get a clear grasp of these ideas is to know something of the circumstances in which they originated. It would not be appropriate in this study to proceed step by step through the history of political representation but it will be helpful to look at the periods when significant movements of ideas took place. We shall begin with the period when representative institutions were first established as part of the machinery of secular government.

This development had of course been preceded by the establishment of representative institutions within the Catholic Church and it is possible to take the view that these ecclesiastical developments were of great importance. However, the central concern of this study is with the concept of representation in relation to the process of secular government and there has been a good deal of controversy among historians as to whether secular developments were considerably or only slightly influenced by ecclesiastical practices. Without taking sides in this controversy, it seems unnecessary in this context to discuss questions of ecclesiastical organization.

Medieval theories

As a general rule, normative theories about the working of political institutions are not formulated until some time after the institutions themselves have come into being, and coherent theories of political representation did not emerge until a very long time after the development of parliamentary bodies in England and elsewhere in the thirteenth and fourteenth centuries. But throughout

22

the Middle Ages there seem to have been two views about the origins of political authority which were not entirely irrelevant to the question of representation and were sometimes referred to in subsequent discussions of representation.

The main division among philosophers was between those who subscribed to the 'ascending theory' of political authority and those who were committed to the 'descending theory'.[1] According to the former theory, based to some extent on the practice of the Germanic tribes, political authority originated with the people and was delegated by them to leaders and monarchs. The task of these rulers was not so much to make laws as to interpret and enforce the customary laws of society. In this view the king could be regarded as the symbolic representative of his people, and this seemed to be the position of those early Anglo-Saxon kings who 'headed the nation, embodied the tribal consciousness, and constituted living symbols of religious and even mystical significance in the eyes of their peoples'.[2]

Such a king might also be regarded as a representative in the sense that, first, he had been chosen from among the several eligible members of the ruling family (as happened in some of the Anglo-Saxon kingdoms) and, second, it was his duty to act on behalf of his people in upholding their laws (to which he himself was also subject). Sir John Fortescue, who was Lord Chief Justice of England from 1442 to 1461, reflected this tradition of thought when he stated that the king's duty was to 'protect his subjects in their lives, properties and lands; for this very purpose he has delegation of power from the people'.[3]

According to the contrasting tradition of political thought in the Middle Ages, the authority of some men over others could only be regarded as rightful if it were divinely sanctioned. As early as the fifth century St Augustine had said that 'God distributed the laws to mankind through the medium of kings',[4] and eight centuries later St Thomas Aquinas expressed the same idea when he claimed that 'power descended from God'.[5] According to this view the Pope was God's representative on earth in regard to spiritual matters while secular rulers were bound by laws of nature which were of divine origin.

Because of the dominant influence of the Christian Church in medieval Europe the descending theory of political authority became the established theory, while the ascending theory was, in Ullman's phrase, 'driven underground'[6]—but it did not disappear entirely. In the fourteenth century Marsilio of Padua produced a theory of politics that incorporated some of the elements of the ascending theory, though his main object was not to stress the rights of citizens but (anticipating Machiavelli) to explain the need for secular authorities to free themselves from the influence of the Church. In England for several centuries one of the strains in the literature of political reform was the theory of the 'Norman Yoke', which has been outlined in the following terms:

> Before 1066 the Anglo-Saxon inhabitants of this country lived as free and equal citizens, governing themselves through representative institutions. The Norman Conquest deprived them of this liberty, and established the tyranny of an alien King and landlords. But the people did not forget the rights they had lost. They fought continuously to recover them, with varying success. Concessions (Magna Carta, for instance) were from time to time extorted from their rulers, and always the tradition of lost Anglo-Saxon freedom was a stimulus to ever more insistent demands upon the successors of the Norman usurpers.[7]

This was a myth which embodied some elements of truth without being historically accurate, and its survival over several centuries is a fascinating example of the continuity of a political idea: Christopher Hill has traced it in detail from the sixteenth century to the nineteenth and he says that 'some theory of this sort may well have had a continuous history since 1066'.[8]

But despite the long history of the ascending theory of authority, the actual development of representative institutions in medieval Europe resulted from the financial and administrative needs of kings, not from any movement designed to increase the political influence of citizens. The first phase in the history of representative government began in several European kingdoms in the thirteenth and fourteenth centuries, when representatives of important classes or communities within society were invited to give consent to measures proposed by the king, particularly measures of taxation.

Medieval parliaments

In describing this development it is necessary to draw a distinction between those pre-parliamentary courts or councils or assemblies that were called from time to time to acclaim the actions of the monarch or 'to give solemnity to certain events',[9] but which lacked deliberative powers, and the parliamentary bodies which emerged when these assemblies acquired deliberative powers and came to be recognized as an established part of the process of government. The reasons for the transition varied: sometimes the king recognized the assembly as representing the realm 'through incapacity, weakness or even broadmindedness',[10] while in other states the members of the assembly asserted themselves in relation to the king and induced him to make concessions to them. In some countries, such as England, there was a considerable period of transition, with councils of the old kind apparently alternating with parliamentary assemblies of the new kind, according to the purpose of the meeting and the number of people summoned to it.

The first assembly that can reasonably be described as parliamentary took place in the Spanish kingdom of Leon in 1188, at which the king undertook to 'follow the counsels of his bishops, nobles and wise men in all circumstances in matters of peace and war'.[11] In other Spanish kingdoms, such as Castile and Catalonia, parliamentary bodies emerged and acquired significant powers during the latter part of the thirteenth century. In England the significant changes took place between the accession of King John in 1199 and the enforced abdication of Edward II in 1327, a turbulent period marked by crises and recurrent conflicts between the barons and the four successive kings, only one of whom was noted for his wisdom or strength.

In France there was a dramatic meeting of the Estates-General in 1302, when Philip the Fair summoned barons and clerics and urban representatives to Paris at a time when he was at war with England and in conflict with the Pope, but the verdict of recent historians is that this assembly 'possessed powers only of a plebiscitory nature, to acclaim the decisions of the sovereign without the possibility of opposing or modifying them'.[12] It was not until the meetings of 1355 to 1357 that the French 'estates' acquired the characteristics of a parliament. In these years the king badly needed money and troops for his war against England but the estates showed an unprecedented intransigence, refusing to promise either unless they were granted the right to participate in government, the promise of periodic assemblies, and some control over the levying of taxes. In a series of stormy meetings these demands were conceded in principle, but they were not translated into practice and when the king's position improved he felt free to govern as before. In fact the French Estates-General never met regularly, though when they did meet they were a force to be reckoned with. For the student of modern politics this whole story is a fascinating example of the longevity of a political culture, for the events of the mid-fourteenth century can be seen as a medieval prologue to the revolutionary attitudes, the conflicts over points of principle, the alternation of radical progress and reaction that have characterized French politics in the past two hundred years.

In the thirteenth and fourteenth centuries there were parallel developments in the German and Italian kingdoms that could be mentioned, but it will be more rewarding to trace the English developments in greater detail, for only in England has the parliamentary assembly had a continuous history from the Middle Ages to the present time. In England the Magna Carta of 1215 is often referred to as the first significant milestone on the road to representative government, but care is needed in ascribing proper significance to it. The Charter was an agreement between the king and his barons, and the latter are the only group (apart from children, lunatics and convicts) who have never been given the franchise in England. The importance of the Charter in this connection was that the king agreed not to exercise his power to impose a tax known as scutage except with the consent of the common council of the realm, to which all lords of the realm would be summoned. During the next century and a half the English kings surrendered the other arbitrary powers of taxation they had enjoyed—Danegeld, tallage, and customs duties—so that subsequent monarchs were able to levy taxes only with the consent of Parliament.

King John was forced to make this initial surrender of fiscal powers by the collective action of the barons, which continued in subsequent decades. In section 14 of Magna Carta the barons promised that their agreement of payment of scutage to the king, if given at a meeting to which all tenants-in-chief had been summoned, would bind those who had not attended as well as those who took part. In 1242 the barons joined in an oath that if the king asked them for grants they would not reply individually, but only collectively. This was not representation, for all the barons were entitled to be present. But representation was introduced in 1254, when the knights of the shires were summoned to Parliament, it being decreed that they must be elected in the county courts and it being made clear that the knights would be empowered both to speak for the whole county and to make promises which would be regarded as binding on the whole county. They were to be representatives in the sense of agents, and their consent was taken to be equivalent to the consent of those they represented.

In the next few decades Parliament deliberated not as one body, but as several. The king's requests would be discussed separately by the barons, the knights, the burgesses, and the proctors of the clergy: they were all part of Parliament, but 'it would be more accurate to call the representative portion of the Parliament a House of Communes than a House of Commons'.[13] However, in the fourteenth century the communes or estates were merged in one body, beginning in 1327, and in 1365 the Chief Justice of England was able to say: 'Everyone is considered to know what is done in Parliament: for so soon as Parliament has concluded everything, the law presumes that everyone has notice of it; for the Parliament represents the body of all the realm.'[14]

The English Parliament therefore emerged gradually, and its early development was influenced hardly at all by theories of representation. Its composition was determined almost entirely by the practical need of successive kings to get the consent of the propertied classes to measures of taxation. It was summoned infrequently, there was little competition for membership, and most of those who were appointed made the wearisome journey to Westminster without enthusiasm. Each session would last two or three weeks, with meetings between seven and ten o'clock each morning and the rest of the days given over to talking, gambling, and drinking. But in these proceedings can be discerned many of the elements of a system of representative government, albeit in embryo form.

In the first place, the commoners who attended Parliament came as agents, able to speak for their constituencies and to give consent to measures on behalf of their constituents. This was thought very important by the king and from 1294 onwards the writs of summons required that the representatives should have 'full and sufficient power to do and consent to those things which then and there by the common counsel of our realm shall happen to be ordained . . . so that for want of such power . . . the affairs may in no wise remain unfinished'.[15]

Secondly, they presented—or as some would say, represented—the grievances of their constituents to the king and his councillors. This was not an immediate development, but by 'the end of the 14th century it was certainly considered the duty of members to present the grievances of their constituents in Parliament'.[16] They did this before agreeing to taxation, a convention summarized in the formula 'Redress of grievances before supply'.

Thirdly, they were able—cautiously at first—to negotiate with the king. Often this was a matter of form rather than substance—a hesitation before agreeing to the king's demands—but at other times real bargains were struck. In 1290 Parliament agreed to a levy of one-fifteenth of the value of all movable property in exchange for a promise that the king would expel every Jew from England. In 1297 'the knights and nobles in one body refused the King a grant of money until he had redressed their grievances about the forest laws'.[17] And in the following century there were numerous examples.

Fourthly, Parliament served from the very beginning the supportive function that is a characteristic of most representative institutions. As channels of communication, they carry messages in both directions. Messages from the people to their rulers have generally been thought more important, in the sense of more desirable, by normative theorists of politics. Moreover, it commonly suits the interests of both the rulers and the representatives to lay greater stress on the function of a parliament as a place where grievances can be aired and popular opinions expressed than on its function of maximizing support for the policies of the rulers. For these reasons, the supportive function of representative institutions has usually been either underestimated or ignored in the literature.

In fact, it has always been a vital function of English and other parliaments. In 1261, Bishop Stubbs tells us, Henry III summoned the knights of the shires so that 'they might see and understand for themselves that he was only aiming at the welfare of the whole community'.[18] The motives of Edward I in calling his first Parliament have been described in the following way:

> In 1275 Edward I summoned knights to his first Parliament, not to take an active part in drawing up the great Statute of Westminster I, but rather to hear and understand the reforms in local government which it contained, and to carry back to the community of the shire the explanation of the new provisions for restraining the corruptions and oppressions of their sheriffs. In 1283 and again in 1295 and 1307 Edward I was undoubtedly, like his contemporary Philippe le Bel, making use of the representative system for propaganda purposes; demonstrating to the communities of shire and borough, on whose material assistance he was bound to rely, the justice of his own cause against the villainy of his enemy.[19]

The medieval parliaments in other European kingdoms shared these characteristics, and by the end of the fourteenth century representative institutions were part of the machinery of government in over a dozen states. Of course, it should not be assumed that this development was in any sense democratic. These institutions emerged in feudal societies, where rights, powers and privileges depended on the ownership of land. When the king summoned his magnates and bishops to a royal council he did so because they were men of power, and when he extended the summons to include knights and burgesses he did so because they could speak on behalf of other property-owners. The most influential members, the great magnates, represented only themselves, while the other members were essentially intermediaries, standing between the landowners and taxpayers on one hand and the king and his officials on the other. Nevertheless, it is from these bodies that the representative institutions of the modern world are descended.

3/The Birth of Representative Government

In the Middle Ages various countries had representative institutions but it cannot be said that any country had a system of representative government. By this term is meant a system of national government in which representative institutions play a crucial role in the decision-making process, so that few political changes of any importance can be made without the authority of the central legislative assembly. This form of government emerged in England in the seventeenth century, in America and France during the latter part of the eighteenth century, and in other European countries—largely under the influence of French ideas—in the nineteenth century.

This did not happen as the result of a slow process of development from medieval times, with parliamentary power gradually increasing and royal power gradually waning. On the contrary, the decline of feudalism in Europe was followed by an age which is commonly known as the age of absolutism, in which royal power was freed from the fetters of medieval custom, was enhanced by the relative decline in the power of the nobles and the strengthening of the machinery of government, and was enhanced further by a decline in the authority of the Roman Catholic Church. In medieval times the secular authority operated within a framework of natural law and theorists discussed the relationship between the secular and the spiritual authorities (it being widely accepted that in the last resort the latter had pre-eminence). In early modern times the secular authority was supreme, Louis xiv could declare 'l'état, c'est moi', and James i could speak of the 'divine right of Kings' to rule as they thought fit. In this age many European parliaments became impotent or were dissolved, the French Estates-General were not called for 175 years (from 1614 to 1789), and it was only in England that Parliament had a continuous existence.

This phase of kingly power gave way to parliamentary government as the result of revolutionary movements and ideas. In England, which led the way, the revolutions of the seventeenth century owed more to religious and personal factors than to an ideological movement, but there was nevertheless a considerable flowering of political ideas. In the American colonies many of these English ideas were adapted to sustain the revolutionaries in their campaign against George III, while the Declaration of Independence and subsequent constitutional documents committed the new nation to a radical set of political principles. In France the eighteenth century was the greatest of all periods for political theorizing.

Although the seventeenth and eighteenth centuries were distinguished in this way by a great outpouring of political ideas, not all of the writers had much to say about political representation. The most philosophical of them were concerned with the problems of political obligation rather than with those of representation, and this is not surprising, for philosophical reflection about an institution normally comes some time after the institution itself has developed. But the influence of these thinkers on subsequent writers has been so great that it will be appropriate to mention their ideas about representation before discussing the ideas of the politicians in each country.

Hobbes, Locke and Rousseau

The three great theorists of obligation in this period were Thomas Hobbes, John Locke, and Jean-Jacques Rousseau. To the question of 'whether the magistrate's crown drops down on his head immediately from Heaven or be placed there by the hands of his subjects'[1] each gave the latter answer: they believed it right to think of authority as something which had been conferred on the government by the people. Their treatment of the problems of authority and obligation led each of them to refer to the concept of representation, and it will be helpful to indicate, very briefly, the nature of their attitudes.

The kernel of Hobbes's position in the *Leviathan* is his theory that civil society should be thought of as having been created by a social contract between people who, discontented with the state of primitive anarchy in which they lived, relinquished their natural liberty to use force to a sovereign authority whom they designated as their political representative. This authority, whether consisting of one man or of an assembly, would have the duty to maintain peace and to enact whatever laws it thought appropriate to this end. All citizens of this society would be obliged to obey these laws, providing only that if a man's life were directly threatened by them he would be released from his obligation.

At one level this obligation to obey the government can be justified in terms of the personal security that the maintenance of order brings to the citizen. Hobbes placed such a high valuation on security that he believed all men, if they were rational, should be willing to recognize that any government which preserved security was acting in their best interests and was therefore entitled to their obedience. However, Hobbes wished to buttress this utilitarian argument for obedience by a contractarian argument, and to do this he developed his theory that Leviathan was in fact the people's representative, having been established in that capacity at the time of the original contract. Hobbes defined a representative as an agent who has the right to commit his principal to whatever actions or policies the agent thinks appropriate, and on this basis it was asserted that citizens of an ordered society were morally obliged to accept and obey whatever rules the governing authority made.

The view of the nature and powers of a representative that Hobbes outlined in this work is exemplified in English and American law in the position of the person who is given power of attorney. If (for example) a man who faces a long illness gives his wife this power, the wife will be able to manage his affairs and dispose of his property as she thinks fit and the husband will be both legally and morally obliged to accept her decisions as binding. But although some representations enjoy this kind of power, and it may indeed be argued that elected legislators stand in this kind of relationship to the electorate, it would be absurd to claim that all representatives are necessarily in this position. Hobbes depicted one kind of representative relationship as if it were the only kind, and for this reason his concept of representation, while highly significant in some contexts, has failed to command acceptance as a general guide to the nature of representation in political life.[2]

John Locke was a philosopher whose writings influenced Jefferson and other Americans who propagated republican principles after 1776, and who is commonly taken to be one of the early defenders of representative government. In fact Locke's ideas about representation were far from clear: he is important not for his clarity or his originality (for most of his political ideas had already been expressed in pamphlets by other writers) but for the fact that he advanced arguments about the right to revolution, government by consent, and the rule of the majority that were subsequently seized upon by politicians as offering philosophical justification for their beliefs and actions.

The two main pillars of Locke's political theory are a belief in trusteeship and a belief in government by consent. Whereas Hobbes had imagined a single social compact in which men established a civic society by agreeing with each other to relinquish their powers to a body which would henceforth have absolute authority over them, Locke conceived of a two-step process by which, first, men would agree to form a society and accept the decisions of the majority and, second, the majority would establish a government to make laws and execute them. This government, which might be monarchical, aristocratic or democratic in form (so long as the majority approved) would be entrusted to protect the life, liberty and property of its citizens. If it betrayed this trust its citizens would have a right to replace it by another. This line of argument was used to justify the English Revolution of 1688 and was reflected very clearly in the American Declaration of Independence. But although it was thus employed by political leaders whose actions resulted in the development of representative government, it was not in itself a theory of representation.

Locke's other central argument was that government, to be legitimate, should be based on the consent of the governed, but there is a fatal ambiguity in his development of this theme. While he started by writing of consent as if it meant the voluntary agreement of each individual citizen, he went on in subsequent chapters of the *Second Treatise* to dilute this concept so as to include the tacit consent that men could be assumed to have given simply by remaining in the country and accepting the protection of its laws.

The first definition would imply that the government would cease to be legitimate whenever an appreciable number of citizens felt it had betrayed its trust, whereas the second would imply that any government, however unpopular, would remain legitimate until its citizens actively revolted against it. The incompatibility of these positions undermines Locke's theory, as does his failure to suggest any institutional process by which consent could be granted or withheld. It can be argued that the idea that the continuing support of elected representatives was necessary to legitimize a government was exactly what Locke's theory needed and exactly what Locke failed (with one partial exception) to supply.

The exception is interesting because it illustrates Locke's dependence on his experience of British politics. He declared that laws imposing taxation could never be legitimate unless passed with the voluntary consent of a majority of the potential tax-payers, expressed either directly or through their representatives.[3] There is no obvious logic in singling out taxation laws in this way, but Locke's decision to do so reflected the experience of the English Parliament, which had insisted on its sole right to impose measures of taxation as a way of compelling the king to convene Parliament at least once a year. Some decades later this attitude towards taxation was of course encapsulated in the slogan adopted by the American colonists: 'No taxation without representation.' Perhaps this exemplifies Locke's contribution to political thought; his ideas were neither clear nor original nor profound, but he lent his authority as a philosopher to a summary of political views that were widely held in England towards the end of the seventeenth century and he influenced the reformers of the following century because, irrespective of his logic, he had said what they wanted to hear.[4]

Jean-Jacques Rousseau is often regarded as the father of modern democratic ideas because he was the first political theorist of any stature to base his ideas on the belief that governmental decisions should reflect the will of the people. However, Rousseau believed in the virtues of what is now called direct democracy, not in those of political representation. In a well-known passage, he declared that sovereignty is inalienable and said that: 'The people of England regards itself as free; but it is grossly mistaken; it is free only during the election of members of Parliament.'[5]

The basis of this attitude was Rousseau's belief that political action should involve an expression of the will of the citizen, exercised freely in relation to each general issue that arose. A representative might look after another person's interests, if these were clearly known, but he could hardly formulate another person's will. This was something a man could do only for himself. Partly for this reason, Rousseau believed that political freedom could exist only in states small enough for all the citizens to meet together, as in his native city of Geneva.

It follows that Hobbes and Locke and Rousseau contributed only a little to our stock of ideas about representative government. We can learn somewhat more by turning to the politicians of three countries in the seventeenth and eighteenth centuries and to the work of writers who were more directly involved in the political events of their time than were the three theorists of the social contract.

English debates in the seventeenth century

In England in the first half of the seventeenth century the debates between political leaders were somewhat parochial in nature and contain relatively little of interest to the modern student of politics. The main question at issue was the balance of power between the three institutions that jointly comprised the King-in-Parliament, namely the monarchy, the House of Lords and the House of Commons. The varied actions which precipitated the crisis of 1640 were the king's attempts to levy taxes without parliamentary authority, the Archbishop of Canterbury's intolerance of church reformers, and the rebellion of the Scots and the Irish. The king was forced to call Parliament to raise revenue to finance his military campaigns, and Parliament refused to give the king what he wanted until other grievances were settled. Attitudes hardened and the country moved into a state of civil war between the Parliamentarians and the Royalists.

In this conflict the ideal to which the Parliamentarians looked was a rather hazy notion of a balanced constitution, thought to have existed at some time in the past. Most of their arguments were cast in the form of an appeal to historical precedent, as indeed were most of their opponents' arguments. As history was conceived of in static terms, with the experience of Richard III no more and no less relevant than that of Elizabeth, the resulting debate was singularly unilluminating. 'Each side accused the other, with varying degrees of accuracy and sincerity, of exceeding their customary rights or neglecting their customary duties', and many of the arguments were concerned, 'not to prove that this or that element of government was good or bad in itself, but whether or not it had existed at the time of the Black Prince'.[6] There were repeated assertions that the Houses of Parliament represented the kingdom in their quarrels with the king but the assertions were not based on a clearly-defined view of the nature of representation and it is difficult to learn anything of conceptual interest about representation from these controversies.

Nor are the immediate controversies surrounding the 1688 revolution of much relevance, as political questions were overshadowed by religious and personal issues. However, the seventeenth century saw the emergence of two important styles of thought about the question of political representation, one being the radical conception that all men have a right to be enfranchised and the other being the Whig view of the role of members of Parliament.

The demand for manhood suffrage was made for the first time in England in the 1640s, by a group of soldiers and civilians who came to be known as the Levellers. Unlike the Parliamentarians, they were not so concerned about the powers of Parliament in relation to the executive as they were about Parliament's composition and relationship to the people. While the Levellers recognized that Parliament was the law-making body, they believed that its legislation would only be legitimate if all male citizens were able to participate in the election of its members. Wildman, an agent of the private soldiers, put the argument in the following terms:

> I conceive that the undeniable maxim of government is that all government is in the free assent of the people. If so, then upon that account there is no person that is under a free government or hath justly his own, unless he by his free consent be put under that government. This he cannot be unless he be consenting to it and therefore according to this maxim there is never a person in England but aught to have a voice in elections . . . there are no laws that in this strictness and vigour of justice any man is bound to that are not made by those whom he doth consent to.[7]

Colonel Rainborough agreed, declaring that 'Every man born in England cannot, aught not, neither by the law of God nor the law of nature, to be exempted from the choice of those who are to make laws for him to live under and for him, for ought I know, to lose his life under.'[8]

In the three 'Agreements of the People', the Levellers demanded annual or biennial Parliaments and equal constituencies as well as manhood suffrage; they declared that Parliament should be the agent of the popular will; and they maintained that the people possessed certain natural rights, such as religious freedom and equality before the law, which Parliament should not be entitled to curtail. But they did not explain what the relations should be between Parliament and the executive branch of government and they gave no clear account of how the popular will was to be translated into governmental action.

It follows that the Levellers' concept of political representation was in one basic respect similar to the medieval concept. The political representative had been viewed as an agent, sent to the national Parliament by classes or communities within society to give or withhold their consent to measures of taxation or legislation proposed by the executive. The Levellers wished to see the right to choose these agents extended from the landed gentry and the tradesmen of the boroughs to the entire adult population, so that M.P.s would represent the whole people. But the Levellers did not see clearly that if this were done the role of the representative might have to change.

The Whig theory of representation

The English Whigs, though members of the traditional ruling classes, developed a view about the role of political representatives that was more novel than that of the Levellers. The essence of this view was that, if Parliament were to be the centre of political power rather than merely a check on the king's power, the member of Parliament would have to be free to do what he thought best in the national interest rather than act merely as an agent for his constituents.

Before developing this argument, it is necessary to enter a caveat. Reference to the Whig theory of representation should not be taken to imply that eighteenth-century Parliaments were divided on ideological lines, with all Whigs subscribing to one theory of government and all Tories to another. Political life was too fluid, too pragmatic and too individualistic to be so interpreted. All that is suggested is that two attitudes to the role of Parliament can be discerned, of which one was taken mainly by Whig spokesmen and the other was taken mainly by Tories. The Tory attitude was the traditional one that the function of M.P.s was to represent local interests and to seek redress for particular grievances, it being assumed that the king and his ministers had the main responsibility for interpreting the national interest. In contrast, Whig spokesmen insisted that Parliament was a deliberative body, representing the whole nation, whose decisions should be more than a mere aggregate of sectional demands.

An early expression of the Whig view is to be found in Algernon Sidney's *Discourses Concerning Government*, which was published in 1698 (some years after it was written). Sidney argued that

> It is not therefore for Kent or Sussex, Lewes or Maidstone, but for the whole nation, that the members chosen to serve in these places are sent to serve in Parliament. And though it be fit for them . . . to harken to the opinions of the electors for the information of their judgements, and to the end that what they say may be of more weight . . . yet they are not strictly and properly obliged to give account of their actions to any, unless the whole body of the nation for which they serve, and who are equally concerned in their resolutions, could be assembled.[9]

This assertion that members of Parliament should be under no obligation to take instructions from their constituents was essential to the Whig view of government. Partly because of this view, the Whigs supported the Septennial Act of 1716 which extended the life of the House of Commons to seven years while the Tories urged the need for more frequent elections. In a debate on a motion to repeal this act in 1734, the Tory Lord Noel Somerset expressed the traditional view of the role of M.P.s when he claimed that as 'this House is properly the grand inquest of the nation, they are to represent the grievances of the people to their sovereign'.[10] Whig leaders, on the other hand, insisted on the need for M.P.s to have a large measure of independence, their attitude being exemplified in the following remarks by John Willis:

> After we are chosen, and have taken our seats in this House, we have no longer any dependence on our electors, at least in as far as regards our behaviour here. Their whole power is then devolved upon us, and we are in every question that comes before this House, to regard only the public good in general, and to determine according to our own judgements.[11]

Edmund Burke was therefore following in a long tradition when he made his famous and oft-quoted speech to the electors of Bristol in 1774. Parliament, he said, was

> . . . not a *congress* of ambassadors from different hostile interests; which interests each must maintain, as an agent and advocate, against the other agents and advocates; but Parliament is a *deliberative* assembly of *one* nation, with *one* interest, that of the whole; where, not local purposes, not local prejudices ought to guide, but the general good, resulting from the general reason of the whole.

> Certainly a representative should keep in close touch with his constituents, and should even 'prefer their interests to his own. But his unbiassed opinion, his mature judgement, his enlightened conscience, he ought not to sacrifice to you . . . your representative owes you, not his industry only, but his judgement; and he betrays, instead of serving you, if he sacrifices it to your opinion.'[12]

The emergence of this view of the role of Parliament was of immense importance, not only because of its part in the evolution of the British political system but also because it involved the development of an entirely new and purely political concept of representation. The three basic concepts of representation, it will be recalled, are:

1 that the representative is an agent or delegate, which may be called the concept of delegated representation;
2 that the representative is typical of a class or category of persons, which may be called the concept of microcosmic representation;
3 the concept of symbolic representation.

Now, according to the Whig theory, members of Parliament should be neither delegated representatives nor microcosmic representatives nor symbolic representatives. They are elected representatives whose first duty should be not to promote the interests of their electors but to promote the interests of the nation as a whole, according to their personal judgement of what is best. This is most appropriately called the concept of elective representation.

In developing this concept the Whigs made no reference to the writings of Hobbes, whom they doubtless regarded as a defender of absolutism, but we may note that Hobbes's view of representation is not without relevance to the Whig theory. If the function of M.P.s is to defend the interests of their constituents the election may be seen as part of a process whereby delegated representatives are chosen and instructed. But if the function of M.P.s is to govern as they think best then the election may well be regarded as an act of authorization, on Hobbesian lines. Willis came very near to saying this when he remarked (in the passage quoted above) that after an election the electors' 'whole power is then devolved upon us'.

During the nineteenth century this concept of elective representation achieved general acceptance in Britain as embodying the correct view of the role of Parliament. Its acceptance is shown in the rules of parliamentary privilege, according to which electors may pass requests to their M.P. but may be committing an offence if they give him an instruction backed by the threat of sanctions. And, as will be seen, the concept has also been accepted in many other countries.

Early American ideas about representation

As has often been remarked, the ideas and actions of the men who led the American colonies to independence were in some respects quite revolutionary and in other respects rather conservative. Thomas Jefferson believed that the development of representative institutions in America fell into the former category. In 1802 he declared in a letter to Governor Hall that: 'We have the same object, the success of representative government. Nor are we acting for ourselves alone, but for the whole human race. The event of our experiment is to show whether man can be trusted with self-government.'[13] And in 1816 he wrote in a letter to I. H. Tiffany that: 'The full experiment of government democratical, but representative, was and still is reserved for us . . . The introduction of this new principle of representative democracy has rendered useless almost everything written before on the structure of government; and in a great measure relieves our regret if the political writings of Aristotle, or any other ancient, have been lost.'[14] But although the Americans extended the practice of election further than any other nation had done, the novelty of their ideas about representation is open to question and worth examination.

Under the colonial system, the British government controlled foreign affairs and defence and also controlled certain lands in the colonies through the governors, who were of course appointed by the Crown. The Imperial Parliament passed laws relating to citizenship, currency, trade, and navigation. The colonial legislatures were responsible for laws on all other matters. According to British constitutional theory these local assemblies were subordinate to the British Parliament, which enjoyed sovereign power over all His Majesty's territories. But in practice the colonies had achieved a large measure of internal self-government long before 1760, not only because the Board of Trade and the British Parliament were generally content with this state of affairs but also because it often took several months for a report to reach London and several more months for a reply to reach the governor concerned.[15]

When George III and his ministers tried to extend their control over the colonies in the 1760s they were therefore attempting to reverse the tide of history. A workable system had grown up which, 'with occasional adaptions to the shifting needs of empire, might have continued to function indefinitely'.[16] But the attempt to impose taxes on the colonists without their consent provoked a crisis which could have been foreseen. The British had the law on their side but the facts favoured the colonists, and the slogan 'no taxation without representation' proved an effective rallying cry. The years leading up to the revolution were marked by a debate in which the two sides hardly spoke the same language, the British talking in terms of logic and legal theory while the Americans talked in terms of common sense and experience and historical precedent.

The Declaration of Independence, which followed the final breakdown of the debate, justified the revolution partly by citing the particular grievances of the colonists against George III and partly by appealing to general principles. These principles were not novel, as Jefferson acknowledged;[17] they were derived from the writings of Locke, Sidney and other writers of the seventeenth and eighteenth centuries who had suggested that natural law and natural rights were discoverable by reason. But the superb elegance of Jefferson's prose ensured that the opening paragraphs of the Declaration would ring down the ages as an expression of revolutionary faith.

The colonists declared their independence of the king, but not of Parliament, for they did not accept that they had been subject to Parliament. In each state new governors were elected to replace those who had been appointed by the Crown. The title was retained and so, after a number of brief experiments, was the general character of the relationship between the governor and the state assembly, so that the separation of executive and legislative powers which had been a feature of the colonial system was perpetuated as a permanent characteristic of American state government. After only a little discussion at the Philadelphia Convention, a similar kind of system was embodied in the federal constitution.

What view did the American leaders take of the role of elected representatives? The first answer to this question is that they did not subscribe to the Whig view which had gained widespread acceptance in Britain. They expected members of legislative assemblies to act as delegates of their constituents, and favoured frequent elections to prevent the representatives acquiring too much independence. Writing of the House of Representatives in 1788, the author of Paper 52 of *The Federalist* (either Hamilton or Madison) said it was essential that representatives should 'have an immediate dependence on, and an intimate sympathy with, the people. Frequent elections are unquestionably the only policy by which this dependence and sympathy can be effectually secured.'[18] Jefferson was of the same opinion, declaring that members of legislative assemblies should have to submit themselves 'to approbation or rejection at short intervals' and saying that the executive (by which he meant a state governor or the president) must be 'chosen in the same way . . . by those whose agent he is to be'.[19]

Moreover, the authors of *The Federalist* assumed that elected representatives would regard it as their function to promote sectional interests and thought it to be one of the characteristics of good government that a large number of these interests should be represented, so that no one of them would be in a commanding position.[20]

While at one level this view resembled the traditional English view to which many eighteenth-century Tories still subscribed, it had of course a different theoretical foundation. In Tory eyes the king was the ultimate authority in the land whereas in American eyes sovereignty belonged to the people. Representative institutions were thought desirable not as a means of checking the power of the government but as a substitute for direct democracy, as a means whereby the people could in some sense 'govern themselves'. And this raises a question. If the English Whigs believed that Parliament could only act in pursuance of the national interest if its members were somewhat protected from local pressures and instructions, why did the American revolutionaries take the opposite view about Congress?

One answer to this is that they had a different set of values. They were far more radical than the Whigs and they subscribed to a radical theory of representation that had an English counterpart in the ideas of some nineteenth-century writers. The implications of this radical view of representation will be discussed later. The other answer is that the United States Constitution provided for an elected chief executive who would be responsible for interpreting the national interest and who would be sheltered from local pressures not only by his eminence but also by the indirect manner by which he was to be elected. As Hamilton put it, the electoral college system would ensure that the president would be chosen 'by men most capable of analysing the qualities adapted to the station, and acting under circumstances favourable to deliberation, and to a judicious combination of all the reasons and inducements which were proper to govern their choice'.[21] This made it easier for the Founding Fathers to envisage a congress which would reflect popular and local pressures more fairly directly than would have been the case had the constitution provided for a system of parliamentary government in which the assembly controlled the executive.

The French Revolution

In France the decades immediately preceding the revolution were distinguished by a veritable ferment of intellectual controversy about political and social questions. It was an age of disconte nt with existing institutions, faith in the powers of reason to indicate improvements, and optimism about the future. As Isaiah Berlin has said: 'Never again was there so much confidence as in the eighteenth century; Helvetius and Condillac, Holbach and Condorcet and, in a more qualified degree, Diderot and Turgot, Voltaire and d'Alembert, believed that they were living on the threshold of a new age, within sight of the ideal ending.'[22] And not only were they confident, they were influential. Their ideas helped to inspire the French revolutionaries and to some extent they 'have shaped the social and philosophical thinking and the political institutions of the western world'.[23]

Of course, not all of their writings were profound. Their collective output was immense, some of them were essayists rather than philosophers, and in the literature as a whole a number of original and penetrating contributions to political thought are accompanied by a great deal of eloquent moralizing. In as far as they were concerned with immediate political problems their main themes were the desirability of justice, freedom of speech and freedom of worship, their main worry being the poor showing of France in these respects when compared with England and its even poorer showing when measured against their ideals. All were in favour of political reform, but only a few of them wrote in specific terms about representative institutions.

Of these, the most profound was Montesquieu, with his acute sense of history and his shrewd generalizations about the ways in which social and institutional factors restricted the choices available to politicians without determining which one they would make. He is of course best known for his theory that political liberty is only likely to flourish where there is a separation of powers among the executive, the legislature and the judiciary. His desire for his own country was that it should evolve into a limited monarchy on British lines.

Helvetius was original in a different way; an early utilitarian from whom Bentham derived the principle of 'the greatest happiness of the greatest number' as a criterion of good legislation.

Helvetius favoured representative government so that all interests in society could have a voice in the making of laws. If some groups were excluded the 'equilibrium of forces' would be upset and the privileged groups would promote their own interests at the expense of everyone else. But it should be noted that Helvetius did not believe that the franchise should be extended to the poor and the ignorant, for he did not think they had any interests worth defending. A good case could be made for the redistribution of wealth by the state, but until that was done the propertyless should remain voteless.

Here, then, were two entirely different approaches to the analysis of politics which had a certain similarity in their practical implications, for both advocated a balanced constitution in which legislation would be controlled by an elected assembly which would represent the propertied classes.

The social and political problems which contributed to the revolutionary situation in France are not directly relevant to this study, but the precipitating factor involved the question of political representation. In 1787 the finance minister attempted to secure agreement to a reform of the taxation system and a new tax on land. Since these proposals were known to be unpopular with the provincial *Parlements*, they were put to an Assembly of Notables specially convened for the purpose, but this body rejected the proposals and stated that only the *Parlements* (or possibly the Estates-General) had authority to approve them.[24] On being asked, the *Parlement* of Paris rejected the proposed land tax and declared that only the Estates-General could register such a tax. In the following year the king issued a number of edicts, one effect of which was to transfer some of the powers of the provincial *Parlements* to a court whose members were nominated by the king. This move led to public agitation and riots; the national exchequer became so depleted that debts had to be repaid in proper money; and in August 1788 the new finance minister yielded to opinion and agreed to a meeting of the Estates-General.

There was then a lively controversy about how the Estates-General should vote. It was agreed that on this occasion the Third Estate should have as many members as the other two Estates put together, but the official line was that voting should be (as in the past) by order rather than by head, with a majority in each of the three Estates required for a motion to pass. Under the inspired leadership of the Abbé Sieyès, the radicals moved in a few months from the claim that voting should be by head to the claim that only the Third Estate counted, since it in fact represented the entire nation.

Sieyès was one of the cleverest politicians of the revolution, who not only took a leading role in the early days but survived to the end, having seen most of his colleagues go to the guillotine in the intervening period. He was also a brilliant propagandist, whose long pamphlet *Qu'est-ce que le Tiers Etat?* bears comparison with the *Communist Manifesto*. His argument that the representatives of the Third Estate represented the entire nation was much more direct than Marx's claim that the proletariat was the symbolic representative of all humanity. Sieyès defined a nation as 'a body of associates living under *common* laws and represented by the same *legislative assembly*'.[25] Since members of the nobility (and the clergy also) possessed legal privileges and exemptions they were not bound by the laws of the land and could not therefore be part of the nation. By claiming these privileges the nobility made themselves foreigners, not entitled to consideration as part of the nation and not even entitled to stand for election as representatives of the Third Estate.

Under the guidance of Sieyès and his colleagues, the Third Estate was transformed into the National Assembly and, having gained control, the revolutionaries set out their ideas. In July 1789 Sieyès 'induced the Assembly to declare that deputies were not bound by the instructions of their constituents',[26] a statement that was repeated in the 'Declaration of the Rights of Man and of the Citizen' a few weeks later. The constitution of 1791 declared that sovereignty resided in the nation, stated that the National Assembly embodied the will of the nation, and said clearly that 'the representatives elected in the departments will not be representatives of a particular department but of the whole nation, and they may not be given any mandate'.

This was the French equivalent of the Whig theory of representation and its adoption marked a turning point in European ideas about representation. Always before the political representative had been viewed on the continent as a delegate, so that there were three parties in the representative process: the principal, the representative, and the party or authority to whom representations were to be made. According to the new theory of the revolutionaries, political representatives were no longer to be thought of as intermediaries of this kind but were to contrive, in their collective capacity, to act as the voice of the nation and so to represent both the government and the governed. This has led Sartori to make the paradoxical comment that as soon as the French representatives were given the name of 'deputies' they ceased (in theory) to deputize for anyone.[27] An English writer may perhaps be forgiven for thinking that Hobbes provided the key to this paradox: the position of deputies in this French theory must surely be that they are authorized by the process of election to speak and act in the name of the nation. But there is clearly room for argument about this view of political representation and it is because of this that so much controversy has arisen about the role of elected representatives in a national assembly.

While this theory was the most important legacy of the French revolution to European ideas about representation, some brief mention must also be made of Robespierre's attempt to gain acceptance for a more radical view of politics. The new constitution that was accepted by the Convention in 1793 extended the franchise and declared that: 'The people is sovereign; the government is its work and its property; the public functionaries are its clerks.' This doctrine had different implications for the theory of representation, but Robespierre's dominance was short-lived and this kind of radicalism did not long survive his execution.[28]

Conclusions

The revolutions in these three countries were in many respects quite dissimilar. The underlying causes were different, as were the political attitudes, the personal conflicts, and the dimensions of the upheaval. But there was an interesting point of similarity in the chain of events involving the representative system. In each case the precipitating factor was an attempt to impose extra taxes which was thought to need the agreement of the existing representative assemblies. In each case opposition on the part of these assemblies led to a series of conflicts and confrontations of which the eventual outcome was a decisive shift in the locus of political power. By the end of the eighteenth century representative government had come to stay (with certain minor vicissitudes in France) in all three countries, from which representative ideas and institutions have subsequently been exported to the greater part of the world.

In this period of political change there emerged two concepts of political representation. The more important and interesting is the concept of the elected representative as an independent maker of national policies, and with it the concept of the representative assembly as a public authority whose power derives its legitimacy from the fact that its members have gone through a process of election, even though they have no obligation to take instructions from their electors. The French constitutional provisions which prohibited mandates and instructions were subsequently copied or followed in the constitutions of most of the countries of western Europe, including those of Belgium, 1831; Italy, 1848; Prussia, 1850; Sweden, 1866; Austria, 1867; Germany, 1871; Switzerland, 1874; the Netherlands, 1887; and Denmark, 1915. Similar provisions are included in the 1948 constitution of Italy and the 1949 Basic Law of the German Federal Republic. The British position is (as usual) slightly less clear, both because Britain has no written constitution and because in a formal sense the British Parliament includes the monarch as well as the House of Lords and the House of Commons. But in British constitutional law sovereignty is firmly vested in Parliament, there being no mention of the people, and the conventions of Parliament make clear that specific instructions should not be given to M.P.s.

The other concept that emerged is the radical notion that sovereignty rests with the people and political representatives are the people's agents. This is the view that prevailed among the majority (though not among all) of the leaders of the American revolution. Thus the second article of the Virginia Declaration of Rights, proclaimed in 1776, stated: 'That all power is vested in, and consequently derived from, the people; that magistrates are their trustees and servants, and at all times amenable to them.'

The preamble to the U.S. Constitution is phrased in the form: 'We, the people of the United States . . . do ordain and establish this Constitution.' And when Washington relinquished the presidency he delivered to the entire nation his Farewell Address which began with the words 'Friends and Fellow-citizens'. Although this view of politics was propagated by Tom Paine and viewed sympathetically by Robespierre, the seed did not fall on fertile ground and the idea never took firm hold in Europe. Radical spokesmen in Britain and elsewhere have sometimes referred to it, but as a working concept of government it is exclusively American.

4/Elective Representation and the Franchise

Before the effective establishment of representative government in Britain, America and France, the main constitutional issues had revolved around the relations between the monarchy and the other institutions of government. But after representative government had been achieved the composition of the representative assembly became of central importance and there were frequent and sometimes prolonged controversies about the franchise. In the twentieth century these controversies are no longer of much practical interest, since nearly all countries with representative institutions have adopted universal suffrage and the desirability of this has become an article of faith, shared by people whose political creeds have hardly anything else in common. But during the debates on the franchise several different views were expressed about the nature of elective representation and the role of elected representatives, and these concepts of representation have acquired a life of their own and have a continuing influence on political thought and behaviour. It is therefore essential to extract these from the debates and to identify their nature.

As it happens, the discussions on the franchise were more prolonged and elaborate in Britain than anywhere else. In France there were two periods of sudden change: the first in 1789–91, when the three Estates were abolished and the middle classes acquired power; the second in 1848 when the suffrage was extended to all male citizens. In the United States the suffrage has been controlled by state legislatures, not by Congress, and the various local debates on the relaxation of the property qualifications in the early decades of the Union were conducted in practical rather than theoretical terms. But in Britain the question of electoral reform was a central issue of national politics for more than a century and the debate (which attracted political theorists as well as practising politicians) achieved a high level of sophistication. For this reason, most of the illustrative material in this chapter will be drawn from British writings.

The concept of virtual representation

This interesting and (for a time) influential concept was propounded by the English Whigs in the eighteenth century and was used to defend the very narrow franchise of the unreformed House of Commons. In that House the landowners were represented by two members for each county (the knights of the shires) while merchants and manufacturers were represented by the members for those towns that happened to have been incorporated as parliamentary boroughs. This was never a system in which representation bore a close relationship to population and by the end of the century the industrial revolution had created a large number of new towns (including Manchester, Birmingham and Sheffield) which had no representatives of their own, while a number of old parliamentary boroughs retained their M.P.s although only a handful of citizens still lived there.

According to the theory of virtual representation this did not matter, for the interests of places such as Manchester and Sheffield were virtually represented by the members for other industrial cities. It was important that the House should contain some members from industrial cities, so that industrial interests would be taken into account in parliamentary deliberations, but there was no need for each city to have its own man at Westminster. This was an entirely logical view, given the Whig belief that taking account of an interest was different from promoting an interest. If M.P.s were regarded as delegated representatives, as in many Tory and some radical views, then their function was to promote the interests of their constituents and the concept of virtual representation was meaningless. But if they were elective representatives whose task was to pursue the national interest, all that was necessary was that they should be aware of the special problems of industrial areas, and the existing members for Liverpool and Leicester could inform the House of these problems just as well as new members for cities such as Manchester.

It is true that as the movements of population increased and the demands for parliamentary reform grew louder, many Whigs lent their support to the reformers. But this does not mean that they changed their views about the nature of political representation. Some supported the cause of reform because they thought a modest change might stave off the demands for more radical changes, while others believed that reform might improve the quality of the House. Sir George Cornewall Lewis, for instance, produced a characteristically Whig argument when he said that 'it is not more expedient that a large town should be represented rather than a small town because its interests will be watched by its own delegate; but because it is more likely to send a good representative to the national councils'.[1]

Representing the people

The assumptions of the Whigs were challenged by two groups of radical reformers, both composed of theorists and publicists rather than of practical politicians. The first group consisted of people who embraced the doctrine of popular sovereignty, mainly (though not entirely) as a result of the influence of French and American ideas. In 1769 the first truly radical political organization was formed in the shape of the Society of Supporters of the Bill of Rights, which demanded equal constituencies and annual Parliaments and proposed that M.P.s should follow the instructions of their constituents. In 1776 John Wilkes introduced the first motion for parliamentary reform in the House of Commons, claiming that the people were the source of political authority and that manhood suffrage should be instituted. In the following five years this claim was repeated by a number of newly established political societies, one of which (the Sub-Committee of Westminster) demanded not only manhood suffrage but also equal representation, the secret ballot, annual Parliaments and the payment of members.

In the same period two middle-class dissenters, Joseph Priestley and Richard Price, developed political ideas based on the theories of Rousseau. Priestley portrayed civil government as having been established by a social contract in which men surrendered part of their natural freedom in return for a certain degree of influence on government decisions. All citizens were therefore entitled to political representation, and could not be obliged to obey the laws unless it were granted to them.[2] Price followed Rousseau more closely, arguing that in a truly free state every man would give his personal consent to the laws. Representative government was the next best thing, but sovereignty would remain with the people and could not properly be claimed by Parliament.[3]

These reformers were followed by Tom Paine, the Englishman who became famous in America, returned to England to engage in a pamphlet war with Edmund Burke, fled to France to escape prosecution for sedition, and became a member of the Constitutional Convention together with Sieyès, Danton, Condorcet, and other leaders of the first phase of the French revolution. Paine's direct style of writing had a wider appeal than that of any other English radical and his books enjoyed a vast circulation among working men, something like 200,000 copies of *The Rights of Man* being sold within two years of its publication.[4] He believed firmly in popular sovereignty, in representative government based on a wide franchise, and in the right of citizens to revolt against other forms of government. While he was not very explicit about either the philosophical foundations of his arguments or the practical operation of the forms of government he advocated, it is clear that he thought of elected representatives as delegates of the people.

But in spite of the efforts of these writers and associations, the doctrine of popular sovereignty never took firm hold in Britain. Possibly a belief in natural rights is alien to the British temperament; possibly the doctrine was discredited in British eyes by its use as a rallying-cry for revolution elsewhere; perhaps the middle classes were too concerned about their property rights and privileges to accept a doctrine according to which all men had equal political (as distinct from legal) rights. Whatever the reasons, this kind of theory—which on the other side of the Atlantic became the basis of American democracy—has in Britain been no more than the doctrine of outsiders, from the Painites to the Chartists.

Reflecting society

However, a different and peculiarly British set of radical ideas not only acquired influence but led to the transformation of British government during the nineteenth century. These were the ideas of Jeremy Bentham, James Mill and the later Utilitarians who accepted or modified their ideas on political matters.

Bentham was essentially a legal theorist who did not turn his attention to the question of political reform until he was in his late fifties. As a legal theorist, he based his writings upon the radical and apparently simple principle that laws were good if they increased the sum total of human happiness in society but bad if they diminished it. By this criterion, many existing laws could be shown to be deficient and many new laws could be shown to be desirable. During the greater part of his life Bentham was content to point this out, hoping that the rulers of the country (whoever they might be) would have the wisdom to adopt this Utilitarian principle as their own. However, during the first decade of the nineteenth century Bentham became convinced (partly through personal experience and partly through the influence of his friend Mill) that this hope was illusory. Ministers and members of Parliament, he came to believe, were subject like everyone else to the rule that human beings try constantly to maximize their own happiness. 'Whatsoever evil it is possible for man to do for the advancement of his own private and personal interest at the expense of the public interest—that evil sooner or later he will do, unless by some means or other, intentional or otherwise, he be prevented from doing.'[5] As British politicians were drawn from a very small ruling class the inevitable result of their self-seeking decisions would be to promote the interests of this class at the expense of the rest of society. Once Bentham was persuaded of this he threw himself into the cause of parliamentary reform.

The purpose of reform, in his view, was to create a parliamentary system in which legislators, in the course of promoting their own interests and happiness, would automatically maximize the happiness of the population as a whole. To this end there should be manhood suffrage, not because people had a natural right to political representation—Bentham regarded the idea of natural rights as nonsensical—but because only in this way would the personal interests of the whole population be reflected in the legislature. There should also be annual elections, to keep M.P.s in close contact with their constituents and to ensure that they did not have sufficient time to develop distinct interests of their own in their capacity as politicians. The monarchy and the House of Lords should be stripped of their powers, if not abolished, and the effective power of decision-making should be concentrated in this reformed House of Commons. If the system were reformed in these ways it could be assumed that a decision supported by a majority of elected representatives would be in the interests of the majority of citizens and would therefore increase the sum total of happiness in society.

These ideas were expounded by Bentham in a number of writings between 1809 and 1832 and they were also set out, somewhat more clearly, in the *Essay on Government* which James Mill wrote in 1820. Mill's basic assumption about human behaviour was the same as Bentham's: 'It is indisputable that the acts of men follow their will, that their will follows their desires, and that their desires are generated . . . by their interests.'[6] Because of this the legislative assembly 'must have an identity of interest with the community, otherwise it will make a mischievous use of its power'.[7] At the same time it must be recognized that each member of this assembly would acquire certain personal interests in this capacity, which he would have the power to promote. To prevent him abusing his power in this way, things must be so arranged that 'in his capacity of representative it would be impossible for him to do himself as much good by misgovernment as he would do himself harm in his capacity of member of the community'.[8] Frequent elections would achieve this end, for 'the smaller the period of time during which any man retains his capacity of representative, as compared with the time in which he is simply a member of the community, the more difficult it will be to compensate the sacrifice of the interests of the longer period by the profits of misgovernment during the shorter'.[9]

Now this concept of representation is essentially microcosmic. The members of the representative assembly are not to act as trustees for the nation, nor are they to act as delegates for local interests, nor are they to embody the sovereignty of the nation. Their essential function is to constitute, in themselves, a microcosm of the nation, so that if (leaving aside their temporary and peculiar interests as politicians) they pursue their personal interests, they will reach decisions which will maximize the happiness of the whole community.

This theory of representation is open to criticism on many grounds, and since the theory has had a good deal of influence it is appropriate to indicate some of the objections that can be made to it. In the first place, Bentham's basic assumptions are questionable.

As a matter of common observation, it is not true that people are always self-seeking, and Bentham's attempt to get round this by saying that he was altruistic because it gave him pleasure is not really convincing. Moreover, the Utilitarian theory of ethics provides no explanation of how moral rules arise in society and its attempt to equate goodness with the maximization of pleasure obliterates a distinction which people in nearly all societies have thought important. It is not only that men commonly think it right to put honour, the keeping of promises, and the well-being of others before the advancement of personal interests; it is also that the concept of morality has nearly always been taken to involve intentions as well as consequences.

Of course, it may be said that the Utilitarian theory can be accepted as a legitimate view of how men ought to behave even though it cannot be justified in the manner attempted by Bentham and Mill. But it is not difficult to think of examples in which the theory would lead to conclusions which most people would find unacceptable. For instance, after the assassination of President Kennedy it was manifestly desirable for the happiness and peace of mind of the American people that the culprit should be identified and that it should be made clear that he had acted independently rather than as part of an undetected conspiracy. Since the chief suspect was dead before the Warren Commission began its enquiries, the application of the rule of 'the greatest happiness of the greatest number' would lead to the conclusion that it would have been right for the Commission to portray Lee Oswald as the sole criminal, whether or not the evidence justified this. It is not suggested that the Commission did in fact behave in this manner; only that the Utilitarian theory would seem a quite inadequate guide to justice and morality in such a situation.

To take another example, there are at present many thousands of Asian settlers in East Africa who have British passports but are not permitted by British law to settle in Britain. It is apparently in the interests of the African citizens of Kenya and Uganda that these people should be deprived of the right to work so that their jobs may be available to Africans; apparently in the interests of the British that the Asians should be kept out of Britain; and apparently in the interests of the people of India and Pakistan that these unhappy migrants should not be allowed back into their countries of origin. If the politicians' assessment of interests is correct, it would seem to be entirely moral and proper by Utilitarian standards for these settlers, who have committed no crime, to be forced into destitution.

The Utilitarian theory could perhaps be rescued from this position if full account could be taken of the differences in the intensity with which pleasures and pains are felt. Bentham was fully aware of the need to take account of differences in intensity and made this quite clear in his *Principles of Morals and Legislation*. But there are both practical and theoretical difficulties about this. The practical difficulty is that it is impossible to measure intensity so that it could be accurately reflected in the legislative process, which Bentham admitted in his later writings on parliamentary reform. The theoretical problem is that taking full account of intensity would mean accepting that there were circumstances in which the objections of one man to a proposed policy should outweigh the favourable votes of everyone else. This would arise in the case of a man whose life or liberty or means of sustenance were put in serious jeopardy by a policy which would suit the convenience of his fellow-citizens without saving anyone else's life, liberty or livelihood. But if it were accepted that intensity could be multiplied by an infinite factor the result would be equivalent to saying that men have a natural right to life, liberty and livelihood, and this is a position to which Bentham had the strongest philosophical objections.

To these basic weaknesses of the Utilitarian theory of politics must be added the practical difficulty of ever achieving a representative assembly of the kind Bentham and Mill envisaged. They used their model as an argument for manhood suffrage or something very near to it. As Mill said, 'the benefits of the representative system are lost in all cases in which the interests of the choosing body are not the same with those of the community'.[10] But a random sample cannot be secured by calling for volunteers, particularly when the job in question requires unusual ambitions and talents and rewards them with poor financial prospects and a very low degree of security. There is no country in which competitive elections based on manhood suffrage have produced an assembly which could fairly be described as a social microcosm of the nation: lawyers and one or two other professions are invariably over-represented and manual workers are invariably under-represented.

For all these reasons, the main function of the Benthamite theory in political debate has been to serve as a criterion for criticism—a standard by which existing institutions can be measured and found wanting. In nineteenth-century Britain Benthamite arguments proved very effective in the long debate about the reform of the system of parliamentary elections. By these standards the unreformed Parliament was grotesquely un-representative of the country and an extension of the franchise could be, and was, advocated as a way of improving Parliament without it being necessary for the reformers to invoke the danger-ous doctrine of natural rights. Successive extensions of the fran-chise made Parliament more representative without it ever becoming, in Benthamite terms, truly representative.

This criterion is still sometimes used as a basis for criticizing Parliament by writers whose attitude may properly be described as neo-Benthamite, since they adopt this line of argument without committing themselves to the Utilitarian viewpoint in its entirety. A notable example is J. F. S. Ross, who devoted two books to an analysis of the composition of the House of Commons (both before and after the Second World War) in order to demonstrate its unrepresentative nature. One of his conclusions was that people under the age of forty were 'severely under-represented';[11] another was that 'elementary schools have less than a quarter of their proportionate representation';[12] a third was that 'rank-and-file workers have little more than one-third of their proportionate share of the membership, while the unoccupied have three times . . . and the professional workers more than twelve times as many Members as their respective numbers in the community would justify'.[13]

The other side of the coin is the occasional invocation of the same concept of representation to defend the status quo, of which two examples may be given. The first is the comment in a *Times* leading article, relating to a proposal to increase M.P.s' salaries, that 'the House of Commons should be the microcosm of the nation and this it can never be if the great bulk of its members are professional politicians'.[14] The second is Lord Boothby's observa-tion in an unscripted radio programme that: 'Ideally, the House of

Commons should be a social microcosm of the nation. The nation includes a great many people who are rather stupid, and so should the House.'[15] In 1970 a Republican senator made a less precise remark in a similar vein about the U.S. Supreme Court when President Nixon nominated a judge who was said to have a mediocre record.

As this last example indicates, this microcosmic concept of representation can be used to assess any body of men who wield political influence, whether or not they have been elected. Over the past thirty-five years a series of academic critics have complained that the members of the administrative class of the British civil service are drawn from an unduly narrow section of society. Professors such as Herman Finer, H. J. Laski, H. R. G. Greaves, and R. K. Kelsall have shown that higher civil servants are recruited predominantly from middle-class families and have argued that this is unfortunate.[16] A similar kind of complaint has been made about the boards of management of nationalized industries. A leading trade unionist has observed that the members of the British Transport Commission do not constitute 'a typical or representative cross-section of British society'[17] and, after widening his study to include the other nationalized industries, the same writer has noted that 'directors of public companies constitute one of the smallest occupational groups in modern society. Yet they have by far the largest representation.'[18] When rioting broke out in Northern Ireland in 1969 many people said that since the Royal Ulster Constabulary was unrepresentative of the society, being composed almost entirely of Protestants, the Roman Catholic community could not be expected to trust it.

Viewed in the clear light of logic, most of these criticisms seem somewhat dubious, for it is not to be expected that the members of any highly specialized institution will be drawn equally from all sections of society and it is open to argument whether they need to be, provided they do their job efficiently. But the Benthamite argument contains a kernel of truth that makes it likely to find sympathizers in any society where social divisions are thought to have political significance. The divisions regarded as most significant naturally vary from one country to another. In England divisions of class and occupation predominate in people's consciousness, whereas in Northern Ireland they are overshadowed by the issue of religion. In the United States class decisions are not regarded as politically important and nobody objects to the fact that most members of Congress are prosperous lawyers. Ethnic divisions, on the other hand, are vitally important and are taken account of at all levels of political activity. In recent decades this concern with the representation of ethnic minorities has even extended to the Supreme Court, which is now expected to contain one Negro, one Jewish and one Catholic member. In Canada the English/French division dominates political life and is reflected in the composition of the Parliament, the cabinet and nearly all official committees. In the new states of Africa tribal divisions are crucial and in Malaysia the representation of the Chinese and Indian communities is one of the central issues of politics. Whatever the limitations of Jeremy Bentham's philosophy, one of his evident achievements was to elaborate a concept of political representation which, in simplified form, has come to play a vital part in the political debates of the modern world.

Acting as trustees for the nation

The most widely accepted view of the role of members of the legislative assembly in France after 1789 and in Britain after 1832 was that they were elected representatives acting as trustees for the nation. The idea that they were agents for their estates or communities or counties had died with the abolition of the Estates-General and the replacement of the old parliamentary system which represented boroughs and shires by the reformed system which, in principle, simply represented the citizens of the country. This being so, there was no logical and self-evident reason why some citizens should be given the vote and others denied it. However, there were obvious political reasons for drawing such a distinction; the middle classes who had acquired or were acquiring power from the aristocracy hardly wanted to share it with millions of poor and uneducated labourers. So in France until 1848 and in Britain throughout the nineteenth century there were debates about the propriety or wisdom of enfranchising people who owned little property or were not thought to have sufficient education to make intelligent use of their votes.

At this point some facts will be helpful. In Britain the great Reform Act of 1832, important though it was in changing the basis of representation, increased the electorate only from 5 per cent to 7 per cent of the adult population. The second Reform Act of 1867 more or less doubled the electorate; the Act of 1884 made another sizeable advance; but it was not until 1918 that manhood suffrage was established. Until that year there were property qualifications of one kind or another, so that it can fairly be said that for the greater part of the nineteenth century the British electorate was predominantly middle-class. The exclusion of most manual workers was not thought to need elaborate justification by the politicians of the time: it was an age when British institutions were believed to be superior to all others and the revolutions in France and the reports of political corruption that emanated from America did nothing to disturb this belief. When justification was demanded it was offered in two forms: that those without property did not have a stake in the community and that the poor were too ignorant to be entrusted with the franchise.

Liberal reformers rarely challenged these arguments outright. Many reformers believed that the franchise should be extended only gradually, while their more radical colleagues understood the fears of the middle classes and sought to allay them. The most notable effort to do this was made by James Mill in his *Essay on Government*. This was published as a supplement to the *Encyclopaedia Britannica*, the readers of which must have been almost entirely middle-class. Mill's method of reassuring them was to assert that the lower classes, if enfranchised, would inevitably take their political opinions from 'The most wise and virtuous part of the community, the middle rank.'[19] His argument is worth quoting in full.

> . . . the opinions of that class of the people who are below the middle rank are formed, and their minds are directed by that intelligent, that virtuous rank who come the most immediately in contact with them, who are in the constant habit of intimate communication with them, to whom they fly for advice and assistance in all their numerous difficulties, upon whom they feel an immediate and daily dependence in health and in sickness, in infancy and in old age; to whom their children look up as models for their imitation, whose opinions they hear daily repeated and account it their

honour to adopt. There can be no doubt that the middle rank, which gives to science, to art, and to legislation itself their most distinguished ornaments, and is the chief source of all that has exalted and refined human nature, is that portion of the community of which, if the basis of representation were ever so far extended, the opinion would ultimately decide. Of the people beneath them a vast majority would be sure to be guided by their advice and example.[20]

Mill's position was that it would be safe as well as desirable to enfranchise the working classes, whose interests would otherwise be overlooked by the representative assembly. But in the *Essay* he deliberately avoided coming down unequivocally on the side of manhood suffrage, saying that it would be reasonable to exclude men under forty (on the ground that older men, the great majority of whom would have children, could be entrusted to protect the interests of younger men) and suggesting in a rather ambiguous passage that it would probably do no harm to have a property qualification, provided it were low enough to ensure that the majority of men over forty qualified. In practice his eulogy of the middle class proved more acceptable than his recommendations. Politicians were reluctant to risk political stability (and their own careers) by banking on the validity of Mill's hypothesis about the readiness of working-class voters to accept middle-class leadership, and when some workers were eventually given the vote the step was taken by Disraeli, hoping that they would be attracted less by the moral virtues of the middle-class Liberals than by the paternalism and imperialism of the Conservatives.

In France the revolutionary constitution-makers established a two-tier system of election with two levels of property qualification. About 60 per cent of adult males qualified as 'active citizens' and were given the right to choose delegates who, in each department, would elect departmental councillors and members of the Legislative Assembly. But delegates had to be chosen from among men who satisfied the higher qualification and these included only about 7 per cent of adult males. This arrangement was not justified overtly in terms of social class. 'The constitution-makers of the Revolution considered that the nation had the right to confer the task of voting on persons who could perform it properly' and 'the property qualifications were presented as the means of securing an élite competent to act as trustees of the nation'.[21] Nevertheless, the consequence of the franchise laws was to give the middle classes an effective grip on the electoral system and this grip was tightened by the first Napoleonic constitution of 1799.[22] It was tightened still further by the electoral law of 1817, which introduced direct elections but confined the franchise to approximately the same small fraction of the population who had qualified as potential delegates under the Constitution of 1791. But in 1848 the Republicans introduced manhood suffrage and direct national elections at one fell swoop, and this system has not subsequently been challenged.

At this point, attention must be drawn to a point of conceptual interest about Napoleon's electoral system. As noted earlier, the Constitution of 1791 gave formal expression to a purely political concept of representation that was new to France, though it was implicit in the ideas of the English Whigs. Under this constitution, the deputies were not instrumental representatives or microcosmic representatives or symbolic representatives but simply elected representatives, whose status rested on the twin foundations that (a) they had been chosen by a constitutional process of election and (b) they were formally charged with the duty of representing and promoting the interests of the French nation. Under the Napoleonic system, the first of these foundations was partially removed, for while the electoral process produced a national list of about 5,000 persons who were eligible to hold office, the members of the two legislative chambers were chosen from this list by the Senate, whose members were nominated by Napoleon. It can be argued that members chosen in this way should not be described as representatives, being (at least in the final stage) nominated from above rather than elected from below. Certainly Napoleon and his close associates were able to ensure that only safe men were appointed to legislative chambers. But their control over the selection process was no greater than the control Stalin and his associates enjoyed over the election of members of the Supreme Soviet, all of whose members were formally chosen by election in the constituencies, and it can also be argued that to deny the title of representative to persons whose election is controlled or rigged from above would limit the use of the term in an artificial and value-laden fashion.

In the United States there was no national debate over the franchise, though there were debates at state level. When the federal constitution was ratified Pennsylvania gave the vote to all adult white taxpayers while the other twelve states had a variety of property qualifications. But these were not stringent in a land where property ownership was more widespread than in Europe, and from the beginning well over half the adult white population was enfranchised. By the 1830s the property qualification had been abolished in many states and reduced in others, so that de Tocqueville was only exaggerating a little when he described it as a country where manhood suffrage and democracy had been achieved. By the end of the Civil War property qualifications had disappeared entirely save for small poll taxes in three northern states. And though some southern states introduced poll taxes after the end of the Reconstruction period this was done to disfranchise Negroes rather than to disfranchise the poor: the poll taxes were low enough to be afforded by most poor whites but they created an obstacle for black people, both because of their extreme poverty and because of the difficulties, including physical intimidation, they met with if they attempted to pay the tax. The poll tax waned after the Second World War and was finally abolished by a constitutional amendment of 1964.

Ignorance as a bar to representation

The other justification that has sometimes been offered for the restriction of the franchise is the ignorance of the working classes. This was essentially a nineteenth-century argument, deriving such validity as it had from the liberal view of the electoral process as one that ought to be dominated by reason. When representation was thought of as essentially a means for the defence and promotion of material interests, it could hardly be argued that intelligence and education were relevant factors, but in the hey-day of nineteenth-century liberalism the representative system was seen as a means for the exercise of rational choice between alternative policies and alternative political leaders. In these circumstances it was certainly possible to argue that uneducated (and possibly illiterate) citizens were incapable of reaching an informed judgement and were therefore not entitled to claim the right to vote. The reports that de Tocqueville and other writers brought back from the United States lent some strength to this argument; American democracy was portrayed as a rough and somewhat corrupt form of government and commentators devised a new political phrase to describe it, namely 'the tyranny of the majority'.

It is fair to say that this line of argument has rarely carried much conviction. One reason for this is that in every society the ignorant are also the poor, and it has never proved possible to persuade them that their exclusion from the franchise was a consequence of their ignorance rather than their poverty. Another reason is that the two writers who discussed the problem most eloquently both came down in the end in favour of a radical view about the franchise, notwithstanding the dangers they saw in this policy.

Alexis de Tocqueville, aware as he was of the blemishes and problems of American society, nevertheless admired the American way of life and argued that the liberal franchise contributed, in no small way, to the vitality of the people. He wrote:

> It is incontestable that the people frequently conduct public business very ill; but it is impossible that the people should take a part in public business without extending the circle of their ideas, and without quitting the ordinary routine of their mental occupations. The humblest individual who is called upon to co-operate in the government of society acquires a certain degree of respect; and, as he possesses power, minds more enlightened than his own offer him their services. . . . He takes a part in political undertakings which did not originate in his own conception, but which give him a taste for such undertakings. New ameliorations are daily suggested to him in the property which he holds in common with others, and this gives him the desire of improving that property which is peculiarly his own. He is, perhaps, neither happier nor better than those who came before him; but he is better informed and more active. . . . Not what is done by a democratic government, but what is done under a democratic government by private agency, is really great. Democracy does not confer the most skilful kind of government upon the people, but it produces that

which the most skilful kind of governments are frequently unable to awaken, namely, an all-pervading and restless activity—a superabundant force—an energy which is never seen elsewhere, and which may, under favourable circumstances, beget the most amazing benefits. These are the true advantages of democracy.[23]

John Stuart Mill was greatly influenced by de Tocqueville's work and based his own case for the extension of the franchise on similar arguments. A form of government, he said, is to be judged partly by 'its actions upon men . . . by what it makes of the citizens, and what it does to them; its tendency to improve or deteriorate the people themselves'.[24] In Mill's view a government acts as 'an agency of national education'[25] as well as an administrative agency, and an extended franchise could be justified in terms of the first function even when it could not be justified in terms of the second. In this view political participation became a good thing in itself, which clearly marks a sharp departure from the views of Mill's father and other early Utilitarians. They had seen representation as a way of maximizing private benefits and looked upon the act of voting as involving a small expenditure of time that brought rewards to the citizens that made it worthwhile. The younger Mill, on the other hand, was impressed with the communal benefits that would flow from a political system which would engage citizens in political activity; he regarded public participation in the representative process as a means of civic education and therefore of social progress.[26]

In the climate of opinion of 1861, Mill did not recommend that all citizens should immediately be enfranchised. He felt it right to exclude those who were illiterate as well as those who, because they paid no taxes, would 'have every motive to be lavish and none to economise'.[27] Everyone else should be given the vote, but to ensure that proper weight would be given to the views of the better educated and more responsible members of the community Mill recommended that skilled workers, foremen and all persons in professional or managerial positions should have additional votes, which would also be given to university graduates and persons holding other approved educational qualifications. This ingenious plan was never adopted in Britain, whose legislators preferred to

liberalize the franchise by the simple method of relaxing the prop
erty qualifications. Almost exactly one hundred years after Mill
wrote, it was officially proposed that a system of plural voting on
the lines he had suggested should be adopted in Kenya as a trans-
lational measure; but this proposal was regarded by African leaders
as no more than a transparent device for maximizing the political
influence of Europeans and Asians and was quickly withdrawn.

In recent years another factor has come into play to discredit
the argument that education can be regarded as a necessary condition of the right to vote. Research into voting behaviour since
1945 (which will be discussed in a later chapter) has tended to
undermine the liberal belief that elections are a process of rational
choice between alternative policies. The extent of party loyalties,
the widespread ignorance about political matters, the degree to
which people reject the policies of the parties for which they are
voting—all these and other discoveries have weakened belief in
the liberal model of the representative process. It remains true
that elections are occasions on which people exercise political
judgement but it is by no means clear that formal education is
necessary for the kind of judgement that is involved.

For all these reasons, the argument that ignorance is a bar to
representation has virtually disappeared from the political scene.
It made what must be one of its final appearances in the 1957
report of the Tredgold Commission in Southern Rhodesia, which
recommended that the franchise should be confined to those
citizens who could exercise it with 'reason, judgement and public
spirit'. The criteria the commission suggested for assessing this
capacity were ten years full-time education and an annual income
of at least £300. In practice everyone recognized this to be an
argument about race rather than one about education.

Other limits to the franchise[28]

So far in this chapter we have been concerned with arguments about elective representation which have sprung from the
existence of horizontal divisions within society. These are, of
course, not the only divisions which have been thought to be
relevant and a rather different set of problems and requirements
have revolved around the existence of vertical divisions such as

those of race and sex. These will be enumerated very briefly as, in spite of their practical importance, they have not produced any significant concepts of representation.

(*i*) *Citizenship*. It is normal to define the political community in terms of citizenship and the only country known to the author which permits aliens to vote in national elections is the United Kingdom, which extends this privilege to citizens of the Republic of Ireland. This legally curious arrangement is a hangover from the period between the wars when Southern Ireland was independent according to Irish law but a member of the British Commonwealth according to British law, but the large number of Irishmen who work in Britain are rarely regarded as foreigners and in this sense the arrangement conforms to social realities.

There is also a somewhat anomalous position in Britain concerning citizens of Commonwealth countries, who are entitled to vote if they are in Britain on registration and polling days by virtue of the fact that they are British subjects, even though they are not U.K. citizens. To complicate the issue further, this would not apply to a Canadian or Indian visitor who happened to be in Northern Ireland on registration day, as in that province a residence qualification of three months has been imposed to prevent citizens of the Republic from crossing the border to vote in Northern Irish elections. But the concept of a 'British subject' has lost much of its reality since it ceased (in 1962) to confer the right to take up residence in Britain, and it is to be expected that in due course the right to vote (and perhaps the whole concept) will be eliminated.

Apart from the United Kingdom, the countries where there are complications about citizenship are mainly ex-colonies which did not have citizenship laws of their own until they acquired independence. Many of these countries are slightly artificial as social entities, are divided on racial lines, or have large numbers of recent immigrants. In Malaya, for instance, nearly 40 per cent of the population is Chinese, and when that country acquired independence a special citizenship law was designed with the object of ensuring that Chinese inhabitants acquired citizenship slowly and only after long periods of residence. Put one way, this can be described as a way of ensuring Malay dominance of the political system; put another way, it can be described as part of an attempt to build a multi-racial political community by easy stages. When

Kenya achieved independence its Asian citizens were given the choice of applying for either Kenyan citizenship or British citizenship: those Asians who made the latter choice retained (for a time) the option of emigrating to Britain but they were excluded from the franchise in Kenya.

(*ii*) *Apartheid.* Modern South Africa is governed on the principle that the state is comprised of several entirely separate communities, each having its own set of political institutions. The white community or nation enjoys full rights to representation in a freely-elected Parliament which has over-all control of the government of the Republic. The ten Bantu communities have no representation in Parliament but each of them elects its own council to control local affairs in the territories reserved for Bantu settlement. The official policy is that in due course each of these will be recognized as a separate nation enjoying full rights of self-government. The coloured community of Cape Province, who cannot be physically separated from the white community, used to have the right to elect four white representatives to the House of Assembly to act as spokesmen for coloured interests, but this right was abolished in 1968. In its place the coloured community now has the right to elect 40 members to the Coloured Persons Representative Council, which has some delegated powers of legislation as well as a consultative and advisory function.

In principle this policy has a certain harsh logic on its side: the governing white community is unwilling to subjugate itself voluntarily to the black majority and it would be optimistic to the point of unreality to expect a balanced system of multi-racial democracy to be feasible. In these circumstances it may be argued that the principle of separate development offers the best hope for political stability, provided the communities can be geographically separated. However, critics maintain that in practice separation would involve an unacceptable amount of human suffering and economic loss, and if this is the case apartheid will not prove to be a viable policy, except as a means of keeping the majority of the population in an inferior position.

(*iii*) *Sex.* In a society dominated by men, such as Victorian England, women were quite naturally excluded from the franchise on the ground that politics, like business, was the prerogative of the stronger sex. The same attitude prevails today in a number of

Muslim societies. In Britain the general emancipation of women at the end of the Victorian era led to the demand for female suffrage, which was supported in terms of all the main concepts of representation. It was said that women needed the vote so that their elected representatives, acting as spokesmen, could campaign for an improvement in the legal rights of women in connection with marriage, divorce and the ownership of property. It was said that they should be enfranchised in order to elect members of their own sex and make the House of Commons more nearly a microcosm of the nation. It was said that their enfranchisement was desirable as a way of symbolizing their equality with the other sex. It was said, in terms reminiscent of the Whigs, that enfranchisement would enlarge the reservoir of talent and experience on which Parliament could draw. Attacked on four fronts in this way, the opponents of female suffrage found themselves in a difficult intellectual position, and when the demand was granted it was probably less because of the vigour of the Suffragettes' campaign than because it was difficult for male politicians to muster counter-arguments that carried conviction.

(*iv*) *Loyalty*. It has occasionally been held that certain categories of citizen who were thought to be fundamentally opposed to the political system should be deprived of the right to participate in the working of that system. This view was taken for a period during the French Revolution and it was the official doctrine of the Soviet Union from 1917 until 1936. In this period the franchise was denied to all members of the former ruling classes, defined to include not only those who had occupied some kind of official position before the Revolution but also capitalists, *rentiers* and clergymen. A further example occurred in Kenya in 1956, when members of the three tribes who had been associated with the Mau Mau campaign were excluded from the franchise unless they could demonstrate that they had aided the administration during the crisis.

Conclusions

The debate over the franchise began in the second half of the eighteenth century and continued until the first half of the twentieth century. It was an essential ingredient in the making of the modern political world, in which (for the first time in human history) it has become the normal condition of men both for their lives to be controlled at every turn by the actions of government and for them to have some part, however small, in the process by which their governors are chosen. The debate has produced a new concept of major importance, described above as the concept of elective representation, together with a number of other concepts which have been examined. Having clarified these concepts by examining them in historical perspective, we shall turn in the following chapters to a more analytical discussion of the problems of representative government.

5 / Representing Interests

Much, perhaps most, of the public controversy about representative institutions in the nation-state has revolved around the question of who should be represented in the legislative assembly. There are, however, problems of conceptual interest about the slightly different question of what should be, or what is, represented. Until the second half of the eighteenth century this was hardly an important question, since it was generally agreed that the function of political representatives was to defend the material interests of the propertied groups for whom they spoke, such as the landowners, the merchants and the clergy. With the extension of representative government in the past two hundred years the question has become important, however, and the various answers to it will be discussed in this chapter and the next under the following headings: (a) the representation of personal interests; (b) the representation of class interests; (c) the representation of sectional interests; (d) the representation of opinions; and (e) the representation of political parties.

The representation of personal interests

As noted earlier, the lead in the campaign for the liberalization of British institutions in the nineteenth century was taken by the Utilitarians, who believed that the object of the representative process should be to ensure that the personal interests of the entire body of citizens were reflected in the House of Commons. In the Benthamite view of society each man was an isolated individual, pursuing a personal road to happiness which only he could define. It followed that so many thousand electors in a constituency would have so many thousand personal interests, and it could not sensibly be expected that an M.P. could act as a delegate for the interests of his constituents. The Benthamites therefore put their

72

faith in the different view that a properly elected Parliament would reflect the interests of the citizens as a whole in the way that a random sample reflects the characteristics of the larger body from which it is drawn.

It was assumed that there would be disagreements between representatives and a constant need for compromise. It was not thought, however, that there would ever be a fundamental conflict which could not be bridged by compromises. This belief in the fundamental harmony, or at least fundamental compatibility, of personal interests in society was not defended very convincingly in political terms but it seems to have owed a great deal to the analogy between politics and economics. Political man was seen as essentially the same as economic man, as a rational, calculating, self-seeking individual trying to maximize his own welfare. The Utilitarians accepted Adam Smith's theory that economic affairs in a free market were guided by 'an invisible hand' which so arranged things that the maximum benefit for all would result from the interaction of persons seeking only to increase their individual profits. A free society was regarded as equivalent to a free market, with the state as neutral in each case, and it was assumed that the happiness of all would be maximized by the pursuit of individual satisfactions. In this way the whole problem of what constitutes the public interest was argued away. That individual Utilitarian writers were sometimes worried about this is clear from their anxieties about the ignorance of the masses, the need for enlightened leadership and so forth, but they were nevertheless pretty well committed to the rather simple model of society that has been outlined.

Now, whatever the merits and limitations of Adam Smith's economic theories, it is clearly inadequate to believe, as a general rule, in the fundamental compatibility of political interests. There are many societies where the interests of minorities take a permanent second place to the interests of the majority, to the extent that members of the minority have an understandable feeling of grievance and political injustice. The most obvious contemporary examples—each of them different from the others—are the Catholics in Northern Ireland, the Chinese in Indonesia, the Arabs in Israel, and the Negroes in the United States, but the list could easily be extended. In societies of this kind, marked by political incompatibilities of a fundamental nature, the microcosmic theory of representation clearly breaks down: a representative assembly of this desired type would simply mirror the divisions in society and do nothing to heal them.

One question which emerges is that of how many societies are marked by fundamental political incompatibilities. According to the most influential political doctrine of the contemporary world, all societies other than Communist societies are in this position, whether or not their leaders realize it. The Marxist view of politics and representation stands in sharp contrast to the Utilitarian view and may conveniently be juxtaposed to it.

The representation of class interests

To the Marxist, the most essential fact about societies is that they are divided into economic classes, each of which is in conflict with the others. In the Western world of the nineteenth and twentieth centuries the essential conflict is between the capitalist class and the proletariat, each of which is defined in terms of its relationship to the means of production. The capitalists own the means of production and thus control the levers of power in society; the proletariat have no assets but their ability to hire out their labour. The nature of this relationship means that the workers are inevitably exploited by the capitalists and this state of affairs can only be ended by the abolition of private ownership of the means of production.

Political institutions and relationships were seen by Marx as largely determined by economic institutions and relationships— as being part of the superstructure of society rather than as part of the basic structure. In a capitalist society the inevitable function of the state was to preserve the capitalist system, and the government could be regarded as a committee for managing the affairs of the bourgeoisie. Representative institutions in this type of society could act as a channel of communication and in favourable circumstances might lead to some amelioration of the workers' conditions of life, but they could not be expected to bring about that radical transformation of the economic and social order which was necessary if the working classes were to be freed from their position of exploitation. In brief, the capitalist state could not be expected to destroy capitalism. It follows from this that representative institutions of a liberal democratic type must be seen as part of a façade which tends to mask the real nature of class conflict and to prevent the workers from recognizing that a fundamental improvement in the condition of their lives can only be brought about by revolution.

Of course, the Marxist attitude to representative government cannot be adequately summarized in a few sentences. Marx's theories were sophisticated; his writings on this particular topic were somewhat ambiguous; and the Marxist doctrine has been developed and extended by a number of later writers. The purpose of including this sketch is not to explain Marxism but simply to indicate that Marxists have a model of society which can be contrasted with the Utilitarian model on almost every score. The main points of contrast can be enumerated:

1 (a) In the Utilitarian view society is composed of so many million individuals, each pursuing his own goals and promoting his personal interests.

   (b) In the Marxist view society is composed of two or three economic classes, each bound together by the common interests of its members.

2 (a) The Utilitarian assumes that economic and political behaviour is governed by the free will of the individuals participating. Some people seek more wealth, others prefer more leisure; some people want to promote poetry and the arts, others are more interested in gambling; some would like to see birth control and abortion promoted by the government, others would like to see them banned; and none of these preferences can be predicted by an observer armed with data about age, sex, and social and economic status.

   (b) The Marxist believes in a form of social determinism. The fundamental interests of citizens are determined by their class position and an understanding of this will guide their political actions in predictable directions. Of course, some people are not politically conscious while others suffer from false consciousness of their own position, but in the long run the light will dawn and people will take up their appropriate postures.

3 (*a*) The Utilitarian believes that there are no fundamental conflicts in society which would prevent the maximization of happiness by compromises and adjustments.

(*b*) The Marxist believes that non-Communist societies are riven by fundamental conflict between classes.

4 (*a*) In the Utilitarian view the state is neutral, though care has to be taken (by a wide franchise and frequent elections) to ensure that its decisions are not biased in favour of particular groups.

(*b*) In the Marxist view the state is inevitably a tool of the class which controls the means of production.

5 (*a*) In the Utilitarian view liberal democracy is the best form of government.

(*b*) In the Marxist view liberal democracy is a sham.

Despite the clear contrast between these two models, each of which is internally consistent, practising politicians have often mixed assumptions from one with beliefs from the other. Thus, in the second half of the nineteenth century many British Liberals came to believe in the existence of a degree of class conflict between the industrial working class and the rest of society, and consequently to express apprehension about the probable effects of giving the vote to industrial workers. One such was Robert Lowe, who warned his colleagues in the following terms: 'While you are dreaming of equality you are creating the greatest inequality, by placing the minority, in which are included the rich and educated, at the mercy of those who live by daily labour.'[1]

Gladstone's reply to this was that they had had two Parliaments since the 1867 Reform Act and while 'both of them have shown, in their respective ways, an attention to the interests of labour which was greatly needed . . . neither of them has supplied so much as a shadow of warrant for the charge that the working men would combine together, in the interests of their own class, to wage war upon other classes'.[2]

This particular kind of Liberal optimism became impossible

after the growth of the Labour Party in the early years of the present century, since the original aim of the party was to promote the interests of the working class by securing the election of working-class members of Parliament. But it must be noted that the Labour Party, in common with many other Social Democratic parties, accepts only some of the assumptions of the Marxists. To some extent (though not entirely) the first three of the Marxist assumptions listed above are accepted by Labour, but the fourth and fifth Marxist assumptions are rejected. It is partly because Social Democrats have never been able to agree upon a consistent model of society and politics that Social Democratic parties have been so prone to internal strife about ideological questions.

One of the questions that has repeatedly caused controversy among Social Democrats is the role of their elected representatives. On the one hand, Social Democrats are committed to bringing about social reform by parliamentary means, which means working within a system in which elected representatives are normally expected to have a free hand in determining policies which they think will promote the public interest, unhampered by instructions from extra-parliamentary bodies. On the other hand, it is natural for a party whose primary function is to promote the interests of the working class to feel that its representatives are to some extent delegates, sent to the parliamentary assembly with a particular mandate. This is a genuine dilemma which emerges in Britain in the perennial debate about whether the Parliamentary Labour Party—the political wing of the Labour Movement—should be bound by resolutions passed at the Annual Conference of the Party, where trade-union delegates control three-quarters of the votes.

Contemporary political scientists have also drawn assumptions and hypotheses from both the Utilitarian and the Marxist models. Most research into electoral behaviour has been based on the belief, expressed implicitly or explicitly, that liberal democracy is a desirable form of government which tends to make decision makers responsive to the interests and desires of the voters. At the same time, many scholars have accepted a form of social determinism when investigating voting behaviour. For example, the several million working-class people in Britain who vote Conservative have frequently been described as 'deviant cases', the assumption being that workers ought to vote Labour. Some of the explanations of working-class Conservatism, made by scholars who are far from being Marxists, have also involved something very like the Marxist concept of false consciousness: it has been suggested that working-class Conservatives are people whose subjective social status is higher than their objective social status, or that buying a house on a mortgage has given them a false sense of identification with the propertied classes. In statistical terms, these hypotheses (if true) can explain the behaviour of only a small proportion of working-class Conservatives, and their continuing attraction for political scientists is something of a mystery.

The representation of sectional interests

Of course, many politicians and writers have a view of society which is neither Utilitarian nor Marxist. To one such group, the most important characteristic of a modern society (as distinct from feudal or peasant societies) is that it is composed of sections and groups with overlapping memberships. In this view, a citizen is seen neither as an isolated individual nor as a person whose condition of life is determined by the class to which he belongs, but as a bundle of interests and affiliations. He is a northerner or a southerner, concerned with agriculture or commerce or some branch of industry, belonging to a variety of voluntary associations, a member of this church or that. This kind of view has been taken by British writers as diverse as Burke, who wrote of the 'little battalions' which attracted men's primary loyalties, Figgis, the author of *Churches in the Modern State*, and G. D. H. Cole the Guild Socialist. In America the same sort of view has been taken by people as different as James Madison, the fourth president, John C. Calhoun, the Southern politician and advocate of states' rights, and David Truman the political scientist. In this view political activity reveals neither a fundamental harmony of interests nor a fundamental conflict, but a continuing series of clashes and compromises.

This pluralist view of society is compatible with more than one attitude towards the functions and role of political representatives. There is, for instance, a fairly clear contrast between the views of Edmund Burke and James Madison. Burke took it for granted that citizens had a variety of sectional and functional interests which they were concerned to defend and promote, and he assumed that they would often expect their elected representatives to act as their agents in this regard. However, he made it clear on many occasions, and particularly in his famous speech to the electors of Bristol that was quoted in an earlier chapter, that he did not regard this as the proper function of representatives. In his view the M.P.'s responsibility to the nation as a whole took priority over his responsibility to his constituents and his duty was to promote the national interest rather than to promote sectional interests. He must take heed of the latter, he must be aware of his constituents' demands, but in the last resort he must rely on his own judgement about what ought to be done. Only if M.P.s behaved in this way could Parliament promote the general good.

The direct implication of this view is that elected representatives must in some sense be superior persons, capable of rising above the promotion of their own and their constituents' interests in order to pursue a higher goal. However, James Madison, writing in the same period as Burke, took a somewhat more sceptical view of the behaviour to be expected of politicians. His ideas must be examined carefully as, in addition to being an immensely successful statesman, he was probably the most logical and coherent political theorist America has produced.

Madison's analysis. The starting point of Madison's analysis was his belief that a conflict of interests in society is inevitable and will necessarily lead (unless the free expression of opinion is suppressed by a despotic ruler) to the development of factional disputes on political issues.

> A landed interest, a manufacturing interest, a mercantile interest, a moneyed interest, with many lesser interests, grow up *of necessity* in civilised nations, and divide them into different classes, activated by different sentiments and views. The regulation of these various and interfering interests forms the principal task of modern legislation, and involves the spirit of party and faction in the necessary and ordinary operations of the government.[3]

Madison's second proposition on this theme is that elected representatives will inevitably act to a very considerable extent as delegates for particular interests.

And what are the different classes of legislators but advocates and parties to the causes which they determine? Is a law proposed concerning private debts? It is a question to which the creditors are parties on one side and the debtors on the other. Justice ought to hold the balance between them. Yet the parties are, and must be, themselves the judges; and the most numerous party, or, in other words, the most powerful faction must be expected to prevail.[4]

In a subsequent paragraph, Madison explicitly rejected the view taken by Burke and his fellow-Whigs:

It is in vain to say that enlightened statesmen will be able to adjust these clashing interests, and render them all subservient to the public good. Enlightened statesmen will not always be at the helm. Nor, in many cases, can such an adjustment be made at all without taking into view indirect and remote considerations, which will rarely prevail over the immediate interest which one party may find in disregarding the rights of another or the good of the whole.[5]

It is noteworthy that, in rejecting the Burkean view, Madison did not go over to what was shortly to become the Benthamite position, that the 'good of the whole' is a meaningless concept unless defined simply in terms of the addition and subtraction of individual interests. Being more of a practical politician than either of the British writers, Madison was willing to accept that concepts such as 'the national interest' and 'the rights of men' had some meaning and reality, even though he might not be able to define them in terms that would stand up to scholarly analysis.

In Madison's view the realistic alternatives were that representatives would either seek to promote the interests of their constituents or use their position to advance their own personal interests. The former being more desirable, Madison thought it important that there should be frequent elections to maintain popular control over their behaviour. This view was in fact shared by nearly all the Founding Fathers. At the Philadelphia Convention Madison and his close associate Alexander Hamilton had thought that a three-year term of office in the House of Representatives (as compared with the seven-year term then prevailing in the British Parliament) would be short enough, but many other delegates favoured annual elections and the final decision to fix the term at two years was a compromise between the two groups. Defending this position in a newspaper article, either Madison or Hamilton said it was 'particularly essential that [the House] should have an immediate dependence on, and an intimate sympathy with, the people. Frequent elections are unquestionably the only policy by which this dependence and sympathy can be secured.'[6]

Returning to the theme a few days later, the author expressed the matter as follows:

> The House of Representatives is so constituted as to support in the members an habitual recollection to their dependence on the people. Before the sentiments impressed on their minds by the mode of their elevation can be effaced by the exercise of power, they will be compelled to anticipate the moment when their power is to cease, when the exercise of it is to be reviewed, and when they must descend to the level from which they were raised: there for ever to remain unless a faithful discharge of their trust shall have established their true title to a renewal of it.[7]

It may be noted in passing that this attitude has become part of the American political tradition and is one of the several ways in which the American ideas about representative government differ from European ideas. Frequent elections to the national legislature have sometimes been proposed in European countries but (since the end of the French Revolution) never accepted, largely because it is thought undesirable that the representative should be too closely tied to the interests and opinions of his constituents.

The American House of Representatives remains the only national legislative assembly in the world which is elected biennially, and the practice has been free from any substantial challenge until President Johnson proposed in 1966 that the mid-term elections should be abolished and the congressmen elected for four years. When this proposal was debated, the two-year term was defended by arguments almost identical to those used by Madison and his colleagues. One congressman put it thus:

It is very useful to have to run every two years, because this compels a legislator to go home, to do what I do, which is to bend my ear as much as I can and to ring door bells, to find out what people are thinking about Vietnam, about the war against poverty. They want to expand it or cut it back. They have their reasons about the draft, about inflation, about economic policy, about a million other things, and I doubt very much ... that I would be quite as assiduous in going back and making these rounds if I had to run only once every four years.[8]

Returning to Madison, his third proposition was that since the dominance of one faction (however small or big) over the others would be undesirable, steps must be taken to avoid this. The steps which he and his colleagues proposed for America were three in number and can be summarized as follows:

1   the establishment of a large unit of government covering a diverse society
2   the establishment of representative institutions
3   the division of constitutional powers between institutions.

The argument for a large unit of government was part of Madison's case for the adoption of the new federal constitution. He maintained (contrary to Rousseau) that a small democratic city-state would be conducive to injustice, for on most issues the majority of citizens would be of one mind and the dissenting minority would find itself dominated and oppressed by this majority. A large state would be much safer, particularly if it comprised a variety of sectional interests:

Extend the sphere, and you take in a greater variety of parties and interests; you make it less probable that a majority of the whole will have a common motive to invade the rights of other citizens; or if such a common motive exists, it will be more difficult for all who feel it to discover their own strength, and to act in unison with each other.[9]

By logical extension, a union of states would be safer than a single state, for the factions would be more numerous and the likelihood of the government being dominated by a cohesive majority would be greatly reduced. Here again, Madison was expressing a viewpoint which is distinctively, indeed uniquely, American. No other country in world history has had a national political leader who insisted on the advantages of factional divisions and the merits of weak government. It is indeed difficult to think of any other country where such an argument could conceivably be advanced. The nearest parallel to Madison's argument (and that not very near) is the now-discredited argument of the Nigerian Minorities Commission that the rights of tribal minorities would probably be better protected in a federation of three states, each multi-tribal, than in a federation of many states, each dominated by a single tribe.[10] Yet—such is the uniqueness of American society—few would maintain that Madison's views have been discredited.

Madison's second safeguard was that the government of the country should be based on what he called 'republican principles'. By this he meant that power would rest in the hands of representatives elected by the people for limited periods. In such a system decisions would be taken by majority vote and it would be impossible for a minority to dominate the government.

Madison's third safeguard was the separation of powers between legislature, executive and judiciary which is such a distinctive feature of the U.S. Constitution. This was regarded by Madison as an 'additional precaution' against the possibility that the federal government might fall under the dominance of any one group. The division of Congress into two houses was defended in similar terms:

> In republican government, the legislative authority necessarily predominates. The remedy for this inconveniency is to divide the legislature into different branches, and to render them, by different modes of election and different principles of action, as little connected with each other as the nature of their common functions and their common dependence on society will admit.[11]

This sketch of Madison's views about sectional representation, brief though it is, will perhaps indicate the eloquence and vigour with which he justified the principles underlying the United States Constitution which he and his colleagues had drawn up at the Philadelphia Convention. The argument was based partly on a theory of political behaviour and partly on an appreciation of the political problems that were likely to arise in a country where factional divisions would have a basis that was largely (though not entirely) geographical. The solution that Madison and his colleagues proposed was a system of representative government that would be deliberately made complex so as to maximize the opportunities for the representatives of minority interests to protect these interests against the wishes of a temporary majority. No minority could be given a power of veto, but each would be given room to manoeuvre and some guarantee that it would not find itself in the position of a permanent minority whose interest would be consistently flouted.

Calhoun's theory. The next writer whose ideas must be examined was an American politician who accepted Madison's views about the representation of sectional interests but carried them one stage further. John C. Calhoun, vice-president from 1824 to 1832 and senator for the state of South Carolina from 1832 to 1850, represented Southern interests in a period when the South was in danger of becoming a permanent minority and the interests which its leaders held most dear were being threatened. His eloquence as a speaker was supplemented by, and to some extent based on, the coherent theory of political organization which he set out in his *Disquisition on Government*.

Calhoun shared Madison's scepticism about what could be expected of politicians. 'I have seen enough public men,' he wrote, 'to come to the conclusion that there are few indeed whose attachment to self is not stronger than their patriotism.'[12] Like Madison, he was sceptical about the likelihood of there emerging anything that could properly be called a national public opinion or common will. 'Public opinion,' he said, 'is usually nothing more than the opinion or voice of the strongest interest, or combination of interests . . . Public opinion in relation to government and its policy is as much divided and diversified as are the interests of the community.'[13] To reflect these interests, political representatives should act as spokesmen for their constituents. Control through the suffrage, he said, would make 'those elected the true and faithful representatives of those who elected them instead of irresponsible rulers as they would be without it; and thus, by converting it into an agency and the rulers into agents, to divest government of all claims to sovereignty and to retain it unimpaired to the community.'[14]

Where Calhoun went markedly further than Madison was in proposing that a system of representative government could only safeguard the rightful interests of minorities if it were based on what Calhoun called the principle of the 'concurrent majority'. He outlined this principle in the following comparison of two methods of taking the sense of a community.

> One regards numbers only, and considers the whole community as a unit, having but one common interest throughout; and collects the sense of the greater number of the whole as that of the community. The other, on the contrary, regards interests as well as numbers, considering the community as made up of different and conflicting interests . . . and takes the sense of each, through its majority or appropriate organ, and the united sense of all, as the sense of the entire community. The former of these I shall call the numerical or absolute majority; and the latter, the concurrent, or constitutional majority. I call it the constitutional majority, because it is an essential element in every constitutional government.[15]

Calhoun took the view that in the United States the most important conflicts of interests arose out of geographic differences and he believed that minority interests could be adequately defended only if proper weight were given to the views of the several states in any decision of the federal government. He asserted that this principle was to some extent recognized in the Constitution, on the one hand by the equal representation of each state in the Senate and on the other by the clause requiring the concurrence of three-quarters of the states before any amendment could be made to the Constitution. He believed—and this was the essence of his message—that it was vital for the good government of the country that this principle should be so extended by convention and practice that a numerical majority in the American Congress would never use its power to pass measures which deprived the minority of rights which they considered essential to their well-being.

Calhoun's particular concern, of course, was with the growing movement in the Northern states to secure the abolition of slavery. The Southern states' protection against this threat to their way of life depended on the fact that half the members of the Senate came from slave states. This equilibrium between South and North had existed in the early years of the union and had been maintained by the practice adopted, from 1820 to 1850, of admitting new states in pairs, one slave and the other free. In 1850 it was proposed to upset this equilibrium by admitting California as a free state with the prospect of this being followed, not by the admission of a further slave state, but by the admission of four more Northern states. In the last weeks of his life, Calhoun made a prophetic speech to the Senate in which he warned the nation that this destruction of the existing political equilibrium, accompanied as it was by a lack of tolerance in the Northern states toward the institution of slavery, would inevitably lead the Southern states to feel that they had no choice but to secede from the union.

The limitations of delegated representation

Calhoun's writings are important not only because of his place in American history and his logical exposition of a distinctive point of view, but also because they point to the dilemma of any political theorist who proposes that elected representatives ought to act as delegates. If a system of government gives power to elected persons and those persons act primarily as spokesmen for sectional interests, it follows as night follows day that that system will only be able to resolve disagreements so long as the conflicts between the sections are open to compromise. Madison's optimism about the political system he advocated was based upon his equation of political man with economic man and his belief that there were no fundamental conflicts of interest between groups in a capitalist society. Calhoun's pessimism about the American system sprang from his perception that the question of slavery was becoming an issue on which compromise was impossible.

Now, the evidence of history indicates that Madison's views, appropriate though they were for his own country in his own time, were simplistic and over-optimistic as a general prescription for the operation of representative institutions in the world at large.

In the first place, there are numerous examples of non-economic conflicts of interest which cannot easily be resolved by compromise, adjustment and a policy of incremental benefits. These include race relations in the United States, Southern Africa and elsewhere; religious conflicts in Northern Ireland; linguistic divisions in Canada, Belgium and India; tribal conflicts in Nigeria and elsewhere. Secondly, there is an increasing tendency for political systems to be plunged into crisis by ideological conflicts which are only indirectly related to conflicts of sectional or group interest. Thirdly, it is by no means clear that Madison's optimism about capitalist society was justified. True, most capitalist societies in the West have managed to prevent class divisions becoming the basis of fundamental conflict, but it is less plausible to believe that this flows from the nature of capitalist society than to believe that it results from enlightened leadership by politicians, 'enlightened' being defined as the pursuit of objectives that have been conceived in broader terms than the promotion of group interests. It is suggested, in short, that although in point of fact many elected representatives may pursue group interests a theory of good government is bound to be inadequate if it recommends this kind of behaviour as the norm.

This conclusion is reinforced by the difficulties experienced by those political scientists who have tried to explain political behaviour simply in terms of group pressures. A. F. Bentley was the leader in this enterprise and David Truman is his most distinguished follower. Bentley, in a spirited onslaught on A. V. Dicey and other nineteenth-century scholars, argued that it was a mistake to analyse political opinions as if they had an independent existence when in fact they were no more than a cover for group interests. The real task of the scholar, he maintained, was to make a quantitative assessment of group pressures in society.[16] Writing over forty years later, Truman tried to follow Bentley's prescription in respect of the American political system, but to explain how the equilibrium of the system was maintained he had to give an account not only of actual pressures for sectional interests but also of latent or potential pressures for general interests such as the preservation of civil liberties and the maintenance of constitutional procedures. To bring considerations of this kind within his conceptual framework he had to postulate the existence of 'potential interest groups', whose activities could clearly not be measured, and in doing this he was really illustrating the inadequacy of Bentley's model of the political process.[17]

If politics is more than a matter of balancing group pressures the elected representative, in so far as he is a policy maker, must act as rather more than a delegate. This has been generally accepted in European ideas about representation and at least partially accepted in American ideas. However, this leaves open a fairly wide question about how elected representatives ought to behave. Many of the answers that have been given to this question stress the representation of opinions, and these will be discussed in the following chapter.

6/Representing Opinions

The idea that the function of elected representatives in the legislative assembly should be to advance opinions, as distinct from interests, did not become at all prominent until the middle decades of the nineteenth century. Many of those who acted as early advocates of this idea took the view that the opinions to be advanced were the individual opinions of constituents, just as Bentham and James Mill had believed that representatives should be concerned with individual interests. This view clearly presents certain problems, for while a man's interests are easy to recognize and relatively stable, his opinions tend to be personal, private and changeable, so that it is more difficult to know how they can be represented by someone else. Indeed, Jean-Jacques Rousseau took the view that this would be impossible, which was one of his reasons for not believing in the virtues of representative government. And even if this problem is not taken too seriously, it is clearly difficult to defend geographical constituencies in terms of a theory of representation which lays stress on the representation of personal opinions. It may be plausible (up to a point) to defend them by saying that the inhabitants of each town or rural community share certain interests but it is not very plausible to suggest that they are likely to have common views about such matters of opinion as censorship, capital punishment or the merits of the divorce laws.

It was with this problem in mind that Thomas Hare, an English Liberal writer of the 1850s, put forward his logical but impractical proposals for a form of proportional representation under which voters would be able to create their own constituencies. To get a fair representation of opinions in the House of Commons, he maintained, it would be necessary to scrap the whole system of geographical representation in favour of an electoral system in which the total number of voters would be divided by the total number of seats in order to establish an electoral quota. Candidates would be able to campaign on a national basis and any candidate who got the required quota of votes would be duly elected, second preferences being taken account of where appropriate. In this way any viewpoint that was supported by the required quota of electors would acquire a spokesman in Parliament, even though these electors were so spread about the country that they composed no more than a tiny minority in any given area.[1] Each elector would know that his votes had helped to elect a representative, instead of nearly half the voters being left with the doubtful satisfaction of having voted against the successful candidate. And each representative would know that he had his whole 'constituency' behind him: as J. S. Mill said, 'the tie between the elector and the representative would be of a strength, and a value, of which at present we have no experience'.[2]

The chief practical objection to this plan is the confusion that its adoption would create at every election, and no doubt this is why it has not been taken seriously by practising politicians. A more theoretical objection is that it would lead to a Parliament in which the representatives of specialized opinions would be completely committed to their particular viewpoints but would have an entirely free hand on all other matters: thus the representative of the anti-vivisectionists would feel bound to press this cause at every opportunity but would have no guidance at all as to the views of his supporters on financial affairs or foreign policy. In such a Parliament it would be possible for the fate of the government's economic policy to depend on the support that could be elicited from a motley assortment of vegetarians, prohibitionists, and Christian Scientists.

J. S. Mill, who was the most distinguished supporter of Hare's scheme, did not look at the matter in quite this way. To Mill, the great advantage of the scheme was that it would enable the intelligent élite of the country, who would be in a minority in most geographic constituencies, to band together to secure the election of men of distinction. As he said:

> The only quarter in which to look for a supplement, or completing corrective, to the instincts of a democratic majority, is the instructed minority; but, in the ordinary

mode of constituting democracy, this minority has no organ; Mr. Hare's system provides one.[3]

This raises the whole question of whether elected representatives should reflect such opinions as exist among the population, presumably in proportion to their distribution, or whether the representatives should pay special heed to informed opinions and should themselves be educated persons capable of leading opinion. If it is believed that every citizen's opinions are of equal worth certain conclusions follow, not only about the working of the representative system but also about the case for popular referenda on some kinds of issue. If this is not believed, the non-believer is faced not so much with conclusions as with problems about the proper operation of representative government.

As a matter of history, it seems fair to say that in the American political tradition this belief is a dominant strand whereas in the political tradition of Britain and other European countries it is only one strand among others. This difference is revealed in the different tone of political speeches in the two continents. It emerges in institutional arrangements such as the use of referenda in some state and many city governments in America, which has very few parallels in Europe. It is reflected in the readiness of Americans (but not Europeans) to persevere with laws and policies which are favoured by the majority even though their consequences and repercussions are disastrous from the point of view of law enforcement agencies, examples being prohibition in the 1920s and the refusal to supply drugs to drug addicts in the 1960s. This difference in attitudes can be variously described, according to choice, as (a) the difference between a full and a partial commitment to democratic values; (b) the difference between reluctance and willingness to trust public officials and politicians; or (c) the difference between an egalitarian society and a society characterized by habits of deference to leaders and experts.

Apart from the Levellers and Bentham (who was in any case concerned with interests rather than opinions) it is hard to find a British political theorist who has accepted the equality of worth of each man's opinion. For all his radicalism, John Stuart Mill was certainly unwilling to accept this. In consequence, he spent some time grappling with the intellectual dilemma that was created by his commitment to the following three principles: (i) that Parliament should reflect the full diversity of opinions held in society; (ii) that all literate and tax-paying citizens should be enfranchised; (iii) that, nevertheless, the ignorance of the majority rendered their judgement unreliable and their opinions of only doubtful validity.

Mill's attempts to deal with this dilemma can be summarized in four points. First, he hoped that if the electoral system were reformed, preferably along the lines suggested by Hare, the educated minority would acquire an influence out of proportion to its numbers and would be able to ensure the return of a fairly large number of educated representatives. Secondly, he proposed that educated persons should be given a built-in advantage by the system of plural voting described in Chapter 4. As he said (somewhat optimistically) 'no one but a fool, and only a fool of a peculiar description, feels offended by the acknowledgement that there are others whose opinion, and even whose wish, is entitled to a greater amount of consideration than his'.[4]

In the third place, Mill argued that elected persons should not be expected to act as delegates for their constituents. He put the matter thus:

> Superior powers of mind and profound study are of no use if they do not sometimes lead a person to different conclusions from those which are found by ordinary powers of mind without study: and if it be an object to possess representatives in any intellectual respect superior to average electors, it must be counted upon that the representative will sometimes differ in opinion from the majority of his constituents, and that when he does, his opinion will be the oftenest right of the two. It follows that the electors will not do wisely if they insist on absolute conformity to their opinions as the condition of his retaining his seat.[5]

Fourthly, Mill believed that participation in the political process would itself be a valuable form of education. Greatly influenced by de Tocqueville's reports on the working of American democracy, Mill argued that an extension of the franchise to working people would result in an 'education of the intelligence and of the sentiments'[6] of the citizens thus brought into the political community. Mill had, that is, a dynamic rather than a static view of the political system. He believed that an extension of the franchise, though it would involve risks in the short run, would lead in the long run to an improvement in the attitudes and behaviour of the masses and thus to a beneficial change in the character of the society.

Impressive though they are, it is doubtful whether Mill's writings contain a satisfactory answer to the dilemma which he himself had posed. It is probably impossible to deal with this dilemma if the political process is conceived of in such individualistic terms. If political activity is regarded as the conflict of individual opinions, in which there can be no automatic guarantee that 'the truth' will emerge victorious, there may be no alternative but to put one's faith in the superior rationality of an educated élite and to take such steps as are politically feasible to rig the system so that the élite will usually come out on top. But the most convincing of Mill's four arguments is the last one, in which he steps away from his individualistic assumptions and talks in terms of a process of social change. It is possible that a more satisfactory treatment of the dilemmas of representative government in an age of mass democracy can be obtained by thinking of representation as a collective process. Two very difficult attempts have been made to do this: one, indirect and somewhat abstract, by the philosophical Idealists and their followers; the other, arising directly out of political practice, by the advocates of party discipline and the idea of the electoral mandate.

The Idealist attitude to representation

The characteristic of the English philosophical Idealists—of whom F. H. Bradley, T. H. Green and Bernard Bosanquet may be counted the leaders—that is of most relevance in this context is their rejection of the individualistic assumptions of the Utilitarians and their followers in favour of a belief in the organic unity of society.

This belief is more common among continental than among Anglo-Saxon writers and it has of course a long and distinguished history. Its political correlate is that on issues which affect society as a whole there can be found—or, as some would say, there can be elicited—a common will or opinion which is of higher value and greater significance than a mere summation of the individual opinions and interests of the members of society. In Rousseau's theory of politics this was to be called the 'general will', was to be distinguished from the 'will of all', and was to be found by a special procedure at a meeting attended by all citizens. In Hegel's philosophy a very similar phenomenon was described as the 'universal will', which would comprise the 'rational wills' of citizens but was to be distinguished from the 'arbitrary wills' which individuals might have if they pursued their personal inclinations without regard to the moral values and aspirations of the society in which they lived. In the works of the English Idealists the equivalent phenomenon is called the 'common will' or 'common interest' and is to be elicited by a process of discussion.

None of the Idealists said very much about political representation but an attitude towards it is implicit in their view of society and politics. Their great contribution is their recognition that there are differing levels of opinion and interest. If so many million individuals were each to consult his own inclinations and make his own demands, without reference to the views and wants of anyone else, the result would not be a country which would be governed by compromises and adjustments but a country which could not be governed at all, except by force and the arbitrary decisions of its rulers. But the Idealists insisted that no society which deserves the name of society is at all like that. On the contrary, it is a community of persons who share certain values and aspirations which are passed on from one generation to another, which shape individual aspirations and opinions, and which limit (though they do not completely determine) the demands which people think it reasonable to present. If such a society is well governed it is reasonable to suppose that the state can be based not on force but on the common will of its citizens. As T. H. Green asserted, 'will, not force, is the basis of the state'.[7]

In this view of politics the purpose of the representative process—as of the political process as a whole—is not to encourage or emphasize a diversity of opinions but to reduce such differences as exist; not to produce a conflict of interests between sections but to harmonize interests as far as possible. The political process is seen as one which aims at the creation of consensus, it being recognized (at least by the more pragmatic writers of this school)

that this involves political leadership as well as the exchange of
opinions about what should be done by people who are familiar
with the needs and interests of groups within the community.
A. D. Lindsay compared the problem of democratic government
with the problem of finding the sense of the meeting, in which
it should be recognized that everyone had a right to speak but
should not be accepted that everyone had an equal voice or that
taking votes was the best way to proceed. 'The purpose of representative government,' he said, 'is to . . . make effective discussion
possible . . . it is democratic in so far as it is recognised that everyone, just because they have their own life to lead, has something
special and distinctive to contribute . . . But . . . this belief that
everyone has something to contribute does *not* mean that what
everyone has to say is of *equal value.* It assumes that if the discussion is good enough the proper value of each contribution will
be brought out in the discussion.'[8]

This kind of view was quite common among British students
of politics from the turn of the century until the Second World
War. There was a fairly general tendency to reject the individualistic assumptions of nineteenth-century Liberals combined with
a readiness to accept the validity of concepts such as the 'common
good', the 'common will', the 'social ethic' and the 'popular mind'.
Thus, in 1911 L. T. Hobhouse described liberty as 'primarily a
matter of social interest, as something flowing from the necessities
of continuous advance in those regions of truth and of ethics
which constitute the matters of highest social concern'.[9] In 1928
H. J. Laski declared that 'the underlying thesis of popular government is that discussion forms the popular mind and that the
executive utilizes the legislature to translate into statute the will
arrived at by that mind'.[10] In 1942 Sir Ernest Barker said that the
real basis of democracy is the 'discussion of competing ideas,
leading to a compromise in which all the ideas are reconciled and
which can be accepted by all because it bears the imprint of all'.[11]

Similar views were held by politicians in all three parties: by
Liberals such as Asquith, Haldane, and Grey; by a large number
of Conservatives; and by a minority of Socialists. Here, for instance, are two statements by the first Labour Prime Minister,
J. Ramsay MacDonald. First: 'The radical idea of majority rule
is wrong, because it is the general will and not the majority that

governs.'[12] Second: 'The actions of legislatures can but express the will of the community—not of a class, or of a majority, or a minority, or a party, but of the community.'[13]

In the United States philosophical idealism found some expression in the writings of academics such as Josiah Royce, but they were less influential than their English counterparts and this mode of thought never became fashionable. Few students of politics have adopted it, though two exceptions are worth quoting. One is George Galloway, who wrote in the following terms:

> A true representative of the people would follow the people's desires and at the same time lead the people in formulating ways of accomplishing those desires. He would lead the people in the sense of calling to their attention the difficulties of achieving those aims and the ways to overcome the difficulties. This means also that, where necessary, he would show special interest groups or even majorities how . . . their desires need to be tempered in the common interest or for the future good of the nation.[14]

Another is Walter Lippmann, who said 'living adults share, we must believe, the same public interest. For them, however, the public interest is mixed with, and is often at odds with, their private and special interests. Put this way, we can say, I suggest, that the public interest may be presumed to be what men would choose if they saw clearly, thought rationally, acted disinterestedly and benevolently.'[15] But Lippmann acknowledged that this kind of behaviour was rare among American politicians and argued that the American political system, with its emphasis on frequent elections and popular control, did nothing to encourage it.

The normal American reaction to the kind of approach recommended by the Idealists has been well expressed by Charles Gilbert in the following comment on 'the Idealist tradition':

> We tend to distrust its ambiguity about leadership and responsiveness, to doubt that the same subtle dialogue and ethical argument are possible in the great society and in the small group and to emphasize, therefore, the electoral sanction and the specifics of instrumental representation

rather than the diffuseness of expressive representation; we set more store by substance and procedure than by style; we suspect that unitary claims often mask sinister interests.[16]

Party representation

It is a remarkable fact that most theoretical writings about political representation have ignored the existence of organized parties. This is odd in the United States, where parties play an important part in the representative process even though party discipline is very weak; it is extraordinary in Britain, where the scope for individual action on the part of M.P.s has been drastically reduced by the development of strict party discipline since the Reform Act of 1867.

There are of course two reasons for this lacuna in the literature, one being the fact that the most eloquent and influential theorists wrote before the development of party discipline, the other being the fact that theorists have found it difficult to justify party discipline. As we have seen, most theoretical writings about representation have been concerned either with the proper extent of the franchise or with the proper behaviour and ideal functions of elected representatives. And whether one thinks in terms of the representation of interests or the representation of opinions or the search for a common will, it is not at first sight easy to justify a system in which the elected representative may be forced by his party managers to vote for a policy which is contrary to the apparent interests of his constituents, contrary to the prevailing opinion in his constituency, and contrary to his own personal judgement about what is best for the country.

It is therefore not surprising that around the turn of the century, when it had become clear that the growth of party discipline was changing the nature of the British representative system, numerous writers of Liberal inclinations drew attention to this development in tones of regret. Sir Henry Maine took the view that it would lead to a new form of corruption, in which parties would bid for votes by appealing to class interests.[17] Ostrogorski alleged that the growth of party caucuses would turn parliamentary leaders into party dictators and upset the whole balance of the

4

British political system.[18] Sidney Low said that the authority of the House of Commons was being undermined and 'its own servants' (by which he meant ministers) 'have become, for some purposes, its masters'.[19]

In twentieth-century Britain both Conservative and Labour parties enforce a fairly rigid form of discipline on their M.P.s, but only left-wing writers have made any serious attempt to justify this in terms of a theory of representation. This is the theory of the electoral mandate, which, in summary, can be reduced to the following propositions:

1   that mass democracy will give a meaningful influence to the electors only if they are presented with two or more alternative programmes of action between which they can choose, knowing that the party which wins will do its best to put its programme into effect during the next Parliament;

2   that a party winning a parliamentary majority at a general election is not only entitled but obliged to pursue its stated aims, having a mandate from the people to this effect;

3   that this will not put too much power into the hands of party managers and leaders if each party is internally democratic (as the Labour Party is), so that members will have the opportunity to take part in the process by which party policies are formulated;

4   that individual M.P.s are therefore obliged to support their party in Parliament, since they were elected on a party platform and their individual opinions (unless they involve matters of conscience) are largely irrelevant.

This theory of representation has an obvious logic, provided its assumptions are correct. A system of representative government which conformed to this model would be one in which the individual representative would be left with relatively little freedom of action and in which parliamentary debates would be set pieces between rival armies, staged for the benefit of the electorate rather than for any influence they might have on the process of decision making and legislation. But it could be argued that this price would be worth paying for the increase in the responsibility of the government to the electors and the greater meaningfulness (as compared with a more individualistic system) of the votes cast at each general election.

This view has indeed been taken by a number of American scholars who have criticized the more individualistic system that their country enjoys and have recommended a move in the direction of the British system. In 1950 the Committee on Political Parties of the American Political Science Association declared that the conditions of an effective party system are, 'first, that the parties are able to bring forth programmes to which they commit themselves and, second, that the parties possess sufficient internal cohesion to carry out these programmes'.[20] In the same report, this committee advocated intra-party democracy and a system in which electors would be presented with a meaningful choice between alternative policies. E. E. Schattscheider, the chairman of the committee, has developed the same theme in a number of writings. Fritz Morstein Marx has complained that 'a major shortcoming in the present scheme is the lack of party responsibility'.[21] James M. Burns has said that 'the Madisonian model . . . has provided flexibility, accountability and representativeness in our governmental system, at the expense of leadership, vigour, speed, and effective and comprehensive national action'.[22]

We have here, therefore, a model of responsible party government to which the British system is said to approximate, which has been justified by British left-wing writers (though not by Conservatives or Liberals), and which some American political scientists would like to see their own country emulate. In point of fact, however, research into British political behaviour conducted since 1951 indicates that although the British representative system is characterized by effective party discipline, it does not correspond at all closely to the other features of this model.

For one thing, the parties do not usually present coherent programmes of action in their election manifestos. They outline their general objectives, but they rarely commit themselves to more than two or three specific proposals. Secondly, surveys of the attitudes and motives of voters suggest that these policy statements influence the voting behaviour of only a very small proportion of the electors. People are influenced by traditional loyalties, by the general image that each party presents and by the record of the government of the day, but not to any great extent by election promises. Thirdly, the record of history shows that election promises are a poor guide to the actions of the successful party after it has taken over the government: circumstances change, and plans usually have to be modified accordingly. For all these reasons, it would be inaccurate to portray the British system of government as one in which the electors, by preferring one set of policies to another, give the successful party a mandate to translate its policies into practice during the ensuing five years. The theory of the mandate may be perfectly reasonable as a set of recommendations about what ought to happen, but it is misleading if taken as a model of existing practice.

The fact that electoral research has revealed the limitations of the mandate theory in this way means, of course, that it cannot be used as a justification of current practices in British government. And this leaves an odd gap. For, as the present writer observed in an earlier study, 'while British political practice is now dominated by the assumption that the Parliamentary parties will behave a sdisciplined blocks, British political thought still lacks any justification of party discipline that is generally accepted'.[23]

Conclusions

In this chapter and the one preceding we have examined a variety of theories about the functions of political representation in a liberal-democratic system, no one of which seems entirely satisfactory. By a process of drastic (and somewhat unfair) over-simplification, their character can be indicated thus:

1 a theory about the representation of personal interests which involves unduly individualistic assumptions about the nature of society, unrealistic assumptions about the composition of a national assembly based on free election, and over-optimistic assumptions about the chances of all interests being ultimately compatible;

2 a theory about the inevitability of class conflict which seems to have been largely invalidated by the evidence of history, at any rate in advanced industrial societies;

3   a theory about the representation of sectional interests which fails to show how policies reflecting the national interest can emerge in a divided society;

4   a theory about the representation of personal opinions which involves a host of practical and intellectual difficulties;

5   a theory about the function of the representative process in eliciting the common will of society which is somewhat vague and optimistic;

6   a theory justifying party discipline and the idea of the electoral mandate which involves dubious assumptions about both the knowledge and behaviour of electors and the possibility of keeping to long-term plans for government action.

There are two possible reactions to this state of affairs. One is to say that the normative theories thrown up during the controversies of the past two hundred years are no longer relevant, in view of the increased complexity of modern government and the increased number of constituents represented by each elected person. This view has been taken by Heinz Eulau, who says that 'as propositions derived from normative doctrines of representation have been exposed to empirical scrutiny, their obsolescence has become evident'.[24] In support of this, he points out that scholars studying the politics of developing nations very rarely use the concept of representation as an analytical tool, because 'they do not find our inherited formulations of representation particularly germane to the real-world problems with which the new nation builders must deal'.[25] After examining three types of normative theory, he concludes that 'our contemporary real-life problems are such that none of the traditional formulations of representation are relevant to the solution of the representational problems which the modern polity faces'.[26]

This reaction is straightforward and can be summarized in a few lines. The other reaction is more involved and will require a longer explanation. Its starting point is the view that it is only to be expected that objections can be found to each normative theory about representation, for it is the nature of political theories to be partial and one-sided—to stress one concept and elaborate a justification for one view of how the political process ought to work. The writer who tries to take account of all aspects of the problem under consideration will end up with a textbook, not with a contribution to political thought. In practice the working political systems of both Britain and the United States (as well as many other countries) manage to accommodate differing objectives which may appear to be incompatible when set out in the language of political theory, for political systems are complex and flexible.

Some insight into this complexity and flexibility may be gained by considering the ways in which the representation of group interests is combined with the representation of opinions and parties in the British and American political systems. In both countries, group interests have spokesmen in the national legislature and feed these spokesmen with specialized information for use in debate and in committee work. A few groups draft legislation for their spokesmen to present, while many persuade their spokesmen to move amendments to bills sponsored by the executive. In Britain it is thought perfectly proper for M.P.s acting in this way to be paid fees or salaries by the groups while in the United States payments of this kind to congressmen are illegal, but there are ways of getting round this law. This form of group representation is utilized in respect of opinions as well as interests, particularly in Britain, where conservation groups, civil rights groups, animal welfare groups and others all have active parliamentary supporters.

As well as working through Parliament and Congress, pressure groups (whether for interests or opinions) work through the political parties by a variety of means, including campaigns at party conferences and conventions, the formation of ginger groups, and vast contributions to party funds. The strength of party discipline in Britain does not inhibit this process but acts as a spur to it, as in a system where a party decision binds all the party's representatives it is all the more important for groups to influence discussions in the party before the decision is taken. On the other hand, group pressures within a party will not be successful unless they can be convincingly portrayed as compatible with the basic ideology and aims of the party, and this need forces the groups concerned to think in terms of a view of the national interest as well as in terms of their own particular interests.

There is a third channel for the promotion of group interests which is now the most important of all. In the twentieth century the massive extension of government activities in both countries has led to the development of direct consultations between interest groups and administrative agencies. Each side needs the other, the groups needing the opportunity to influence the officials and the agencies needing both the specialized knowledge that the groups possess and (in many cases) the support that the groups can promise. This practice has become an accepted part of the political process in both countries, as was recognized in Britain as long ago as 1918, when the Haldane Committee on the Machinery of Government reported in the following terms:

> The preservation of the full responsibility of Ministers for executive action will not, in our opinion, ensure that the cause of administration will secure and retain public confidence, unless it is recognised as an obligation upon departments to avail themselves of the advice and assistance of advisory bodies so constituted as to make available the knowledge and experience of all sections of the community affected by the activities of the department.[27]

The development of this system of consultation has led to the emergence of new conventions about representation. Each government department and agency has criteria for determining whether the interest represented by a group is (in British terminology) 'an affected interest', with a legitimate right to be consulted. Some large and important groups are excluded by these criteria: thus the Ministry of Defence does not consult the Campaign for Nuclear Disarmament about defence policy. Some groups are excluded for a time but then win the right to be consulted, as the National Union of Students has won the right to be consulted about some aspects of the government's policy towards British universities. If an affected interest is represented by two or three rival groups, the department has to decide whether they should be given equal rights and whether they should be consulted jointly or separately. If an affected interest has no organized group to represent it, the government may take steps to encourage the emergence of such a group. In some circumstances the government may intervene to the extent of creating a group, the clearest example in Britain being the Cotton Board, an independent organization created by statute to which all firms engaged in the cotton industry are compelled by law to subscribe. A slightly different example is the University Grants Committee, a body composed of academics which was created by the government to carry out the invidious task of deciding how the public funds made available for the universities should be divided between them. Developments of a similar kind have taken place in the United States, where scholars have drawn attention to the phenomenon of 'clientalism', whereby government agencies become partially dependent on their client groups for mobilizing public support for agency policies and the continuance of a high level of appropriations for the agency's expenses.

These examples illustrate the complexity of representative systems in their actual operation. In practice it is rarely a question of whether a system serves this function or that, because in most cases it serves both. Nor are groups or individuals presented with an 'either-or' problem if they want to exert influence, for a variety of channels are open to them. As an example, consider the position of a British teacher who supports the Labour Party and has strong opinions about vivisection and the abortion laws. As an elector he will be represented by his constituency M.P., whether or not this M.P. belongs to the Labour Party. As a party member he will regard Labour leaders, and perhaps all Labour M.P.s, as being in a rather different sense his representatives. As a holder of particular opinions he will feel himself represented by the Anti-Vivisection Society, the Abortion Law Reform Society, and those politicians (of whatever party) who act as spokesmen for these groups. As a teacher he will have interests that are represented by the National Union of Teachers, which will be engaged in constant negotiations and consultations with the Department of Education and the local education authorities; will probably be trying to persuade one of the political parties to embrace N.U.T. policies in its next election manifesto; and will certainly be paying fees to a number of M.P.s who customarily speak on educational matters in Parliament.

In the British political system this imaginary teacher is thus represented in four or five different ways. These different types of political representation reinforce one another and interact to comprise the representation system as a whole. However, it is necessary to separate them out for the purposes of justification (by normative theories), investigation (by empirical research), and illustration (by the construction of models). The process of separation produces a number of concepts of representation, each of which relates to one aspect of practice and each of which is of only limited validity. There is no intellectual process which will enable these concepts to be combined into one super-concept which can be called 'the true nature of representation', for this does not exist as an abstraction and can be found only in the complexity of the living historical process. But an analysis of the concepts is a necessary step towards an understanding of this historical process, not only for purposes of clarification but also because the concepts, once enunciated, feed back into the process by shaping the expectations of participants about the roles which they and their fellow-politicians should play.

In this view of the relations between political theory and practice the traditional theories of representation are by no means irrelevant to modern practice, for they have not only helped to determine the nature of that practice but they have also provided the language in which we understand it. Nevertheless, it is clear that the traditional theories are somewhat limited in nature, having nearly all been developed during a particular era of world history (from about 1770 to 1900) which we can now look back on as 'the age of liberalization'. To overcome these limitations it is necessary to look at the functions of political representation in a broader perspective, which will be attempted in the next chapter.

7 / The Functions of Representation

Normative theories of representation have nearly all been formulated to serve practical purposes, such as the justification of existing institutions or the promotion of political reforms. Most of the theories so far discussed emerged out of the debates on the American and French revolutions and the protracted discussions on the reform of Parliament and the extension of the franchise in Britain. The main political developments of the twentieth century —the growth of party discipline, the extension of government activities, the rise of one-party states and totalitarian systems, the emergence of the new states of the third world, the spread of violence—have given rise to a variety of theoretical writings but not to new theories of representation, with the one exception of the theory of responsible party government considered in the previous chapter. Because of this, the functions of political representation are normally discussed in a language which is slightly dated in character and tends to reflect the values of nineteenth-century liberalism. To overcome these limitations it is necessary for the student to disengage himself from the assumptions of liberal democracy and consider the issues in a broader perspective and a more analytical manner.

One scholar who has done this is David Apter, who has attempted to construct a theory of representation which is applicable equally to democratic and non-democratic systems, operating in societies at all stages of economic and political development. In Apter's formulation, the functions of political representation are defined as follows:

1 *Central control:* the ordered maintenance of discipline in a political system on a day-to-day basis.
2 *Goal specification:* the identification and priority ranking of policies; hence, a sharing in policy formulation on the basis of a longer term.

3 *Institutional coherence:* the continuous review, reformulation, and adaptation of the fit between boundaries of sub-systems, including the regulation of overlapping jurisdictions, and including as well, ideological adjustment.[1]

Unfortunately, these definitions are so wide in scope that they do not distinguish between the functions of representation and the functions of other elements in the political process. Central control, as defined here, is either a function of government as a whole or the function of a government's law-enforcement agencies: the business of public officials and policemen rather than of representatives. Goal specification is a function of all those concerned with policy making, whether or not they are representatives. Institutional coherence is one of the goals of policy makers, whoever they are. The definitions might apply to the role of the Communist Party in Russia or China, or a mobilizing party in a new state like Nkrumah's party in Ghana, but they cannot serve to distinguish the functions of representative processes from other processes in all kinds of political system.

Given that political representation fulfils a variety of functions, it is suggested that a two-stage classification may be helpful, in which three broadly-defined general functions are sub-divided into a larger number of specific functions, it being accepted that not all representative systems fulfil all the functions that they might fulfil. The general functions may be defined as follows:

1 *Popular control:* to provide for a degree of popular control over the government.
2 *Leadership:* to provide for leadership and responsibility in decision making.
3 *System maintenance:* to contribute towards the maintenance and smooth running of the political system by enlisting the support of citizens.

The specific functions may be defined as follows:

1 (*a*) *Responsiveness:* to ensure that decision makers are responsive to the interest and opinions of the public.
  (*b*) *Accountability:* to provide a way of holding political leaders publicly accountable for their actions.

(c) *Peaceful change:* to provide a mechanism for re-placing one set of leaders by another without violence.

2 (a) *Leadership:* to provide for the recruitment of political leaders and the mobilization of support for them.

(b) *Responsibility:* to encourage political leaders to pursue long-term national interests as well as reacting to immediate pressures.

3 (a) *Legitimation:* to endow the government with a particular kind of legitimacy.

(b) *Consent:* to provide channels of communication through which the government can mobilize consent to particular policies.

(c) *Relief of pressure:* to provide a safety valve through which aggrieved citizens can blow off steam and to disarm potential revolutionaries by engaging them in constitutional forms of activity.

It is suggested that a fully developed representative system will perform all of these functions, though the precise methods will vary from one system to another. Of course, most countries have representative systems which are only partially developed. For instance, the representative system of the u.s.s.r. provides effectively for leadership, responsibility, legitimation and consent, but it is not very effective in the other four functions. Even systems which may be described as fully representative vary in their relative strengths. Thus, most observers would agree that the representative system of the Fourth Republic was more effective than that of the Fifth Republic in providing for responsiveness and peaceful change, but less effective in providing for leadership, responsibility and consent. It would in principle be possible to construct a profile for each representative system illustrating the way in which it fulfils these eight functions, though the extreme difficulty of measuring performance along these dimensions means that this would inevitably have to be based more on historical judgement than on quantitative research.

It will now be appropriate to consider the nature of these eight functions of political representation a little more fully.

Popular control

The main aim of liberal reformers in the past two centuries has been to use or to establish representative institutions in order to extend popular control over the actions of legislators and administrators. The achievement of a reasonable degree of control of this type is generally regarded as the essence of liberal democracy. As Mayo puts it: 'a political system is democratic to the extent that the decision-makers are under effective popular control'.[2] As we have seen in earlier chapters, much of the debate has turned on what Wahlke and Eulau have called the focus of representation:[3] to be specific, on the question of whether the need is to represent opinions or interests, individuals or groups, localities or the whole nation. But two other issues cut across the debate and must be taken account of in any theory of representation. One is the question of whether representatives are (or should be) concerned with the felt wants or the real needs of their constituents. The other is whether the control is (or should be) exercised before the event, by pressures and instructions, or after the event, by a system of public accountability.

The question of felt wants *versus* real needs has haunted political discussion ever since Rousseau distinguished between the particular will and the real will of citizens. Some democratic theorists of a Benthamite disposition have taken the view that actual, observable wishes and interests alone have reality, feeling that talk of a real will, like talk of a national interest, serves mainly to justify the tendency of political élites to impose their view of what is desirable on the whole country. But experience suggests that this view is too simple to be adequate.

In the first place, it has been shown time and time again that there is a wide range of political questions on which the majority of people have no settled views. To be sure, doorstep interviews can sometimes elicit a reaction from people who had no clear view before the interview was conducted, but such reactions do not survive the test of detailed probing by supplementary questions. Secondly, people's immediate wishes are often inconsistent. To take only the most obvious example, most people would vote for reduced taxes and increased government expenditures, which would add up to a budgetary deficit, but would vote against the inflation that this would cause. Representatives who felt themselves bound to promote only the immediate wishes of their constituents would find that on some issues they had guidance from only a minority, on others they had guidance that was clearly inconsistent, and on others again they had conflicting demands from different sections of the constituency. If political representation were solely of this kind the ineffectiveness of the representatives would probably mean that administrators and other non-representative persons would play a dominant role in the process of policy formation.

In fact most representatives do not feel themselves bound in this way. Thus, at the time of writing (1970) most British M.P.s are supporting the government's application to join the Common Market, in spite of the fact that opinion polls show a majority against the move, because the M.P.s believe that in the long run membership will benefit the nation. Equally, M.P.s supported the move to decimalize the currency not because this was wanted by the public but because it was thought that when people got used to it they would prefer it to the system of pounds, shillings and pence. Even on those fairly rare occasions when M.P.s have a free vote on legislative proposals they do not necessarily feel bound to follow the expressed wishes of their constituents. Thus, capital punishment was abolished on a free vote when the polls showed a majority in favour of retention, the M.P.s acting partly on the belief that they had a duty to exercise moral and political leadership on this issue and partly on the belief that abolition would show that public fears about the loss of a deterrent to murder were unfounded. It was widely believed that if only the public had a better understanding of the psychology of murderers the public would be in favour of abolition, so that M.P.s who supported the reform could be said to be acting in accordance with the 'real will' of the people; i.e. with what the people would want if only they were better informed and could free themselves of irrelevant prejudices.

In spite of the somewhat different political traditions of the United States, many American legislators also feel free to act on their own judgement of what is best for the people they represent. In their study of the role perceptions of representatives in four state legislatures, John Wahlke and his colleagues classified their respondents as delegates if they believed they should follow the expressed wishes of their constituents, as trustees if they believed they should act on their own judgement, and as 'politicos' if their views contained a mixture of these beliefs. In seven of the eight legislative chambers a clear majority of those interviewed were classified as trustees.[4] In the justifications offered for this attitude, one common theme was the ignorance of the average voter. As one representative put it: 'People are not capable to tell me what to do—not because they are stupid, but because they have limited access to the facts. If they had the facts, their decision would be the same.'[5]

It is therefore arguable that the idea of responsiveness to public opinions and interests should be extended to include something wider than responsiveness to the day-by-day expressions of public attitudes. It is difficult to find a satisfactory term by which to describe this, as the concept of a 'real will' has philosophical connotations to which many people object. Roland Pennock has attempted to deal with the problem by distinguishing between people's desires and people's interests.

> The distinction I am intending to make between 'desire' and 'interest' is the distinction between what is immediately demanded and what in the long run, with the benefit of hindsight, would have been preferred or would have contributed to the development of the individual into a person capable of making responsible decisions.[6]

The distinction is well drawn but it is doubtful whether the suggested terminology is helpful, because there are immediate and long-run interests just as there are immediate and long-run desires. Thus, a firm which applied for a bank loan to finance a new development would have an immediate interest in a favourable reply, but if the projected development were commercially unsound the long-term interests of the firm would be better protected by a refusal on the part of the bank.

However, the problem here is only a problem of terminology and does not reflect any basic confusion. The distinction can be expressed quite clearly in a paragraph, but there is no single word which can be used to denote it without ambiguity. If political science were a different kind of subject a new term or mathematical symbol could be coined for the purpose, but as things are the best course is simply to spell out the distinction in ordinary language. Almost everyone would agree that policy makers have a duty to take account of enlightened opinions and long-term interests as well as to respond to the immediate demands that are put to them. Some say that the concept of responsiveness should be stretched to include both kinds of response while others would say that the concept of responsiveness should relate only to expressed demands and opinions and the wider function should be considered under another heading, which is best called responsibility. From the point of view of empirical research the second alternative is certainly preferable, for expressed demands can be observed and perhaps measured while long-term interests can only be assessed and may always be a matter of controversy. For clarity in research design and analysis it is therefore desirable to keep to a narrow definition of responsiveness, but without falling into the trap of assuming that this is necessarily more important than the other functions of representation.

The other question about popular control that must be mentioned is the question of when and how it is to be exercised. On this question people fall into three main groups. One group believes that the essence of popular control is control exercised in advance, by pressures or instructions or party programmes. Interest groups which appoint representatives to act as spokesmen clearly fall into this category. So do delegates to the Annual Conference of the Labour Party who regularly demand that conference decisions should be accepted as binding by the party's leaders in Parliament. Those American legislators who see themselves as delegates for their districts regard it as a necessary part of the democratic process that representatives should do their best to find out what their voters want and then do their best to achieve these aims. In the days when U.S. senators were appointed by state legislatures it was quite common and considered quite proper for the senators to be given instructions on the line they should take. All politicians and writers who subscribe to the doctrine of the electoral mandate believe that the party programme, once endorsed by the electorate, should provide instructions and terms of reference for the incoming government.

Now, there can be no doubt that some kinds of representation lend themselves to control in advance. This is the case with all representatives who are appointed to act as agents, such as ambassadors and attorneys and spokesmen for pressure groups. The modern practice of consulting affected groups before drafting legislation means that there is ample opportunity for interested parties to instruct their representatives as to the line they should adopt.

However, elected representatives in a national legislature cannot normally be controlled in advance by their electors, for all the reasons given earlier. The only effective sanction on their behaviour, it is commonly argued, is that they face the risk of losing the next election if their decisions prove to be unpopular. On this argument the essence of popular control (and therefore the essence of democracy) is that legislators and ministers are accountable to the public for what they do while in office. The nature of this accountability clearly varies according to the nature of the party system. In a system characterized by loose discipline, such as the American system, elected persons may be held to account for their individual behaviour by published analyses of their voting records in Congress or a state assembly. In a disciplined party system with only two main parties, such as the British system, it is the government of the day which is held to account for its behaviour, with individual M.P.s having to accept the consequent loss or gain of popularity largely irrespective of their personal attitudes and behaviour. In a partially disciplined party system with several main parties, such as that of the Fourth Republic, the line of accountability is far from clear.

It has sometimes been argued that even this theory of popular control assumes too much. According to Joseph Schumpeter, defenders of liberal democracy should abandon the claim that the public is able to control or even to influence the actions of government and should fall back on the more modest and realistic claim that the system of competitive elections enables the public to choose between rival teams of political leaders. In Schumpeter's definition, the democratic method 'is that institutional arrangement for arriving at political decisions in which individuals acquire the power to decide by means of a competitive struggle for the people's vote'.[7]

One of Schumpeter's arguments is that democratic and representative systems of government can be distinguished more clearly from other systems in terms of processes than in terms of achievements. There are historical examples, he says, of dictatorial systems that served the will of the people better than some democratic systems have done. Certainly there have been dictators who claimed to be representatives: thus Adolf Hitler once declared, 'My pride is that I know no statesman in the world who with greater right than I can say that he is the representative of his people.'[8] Schumpeter put forward six other arguments, all of which are impressive, though as he was concerned with the definition of democracy rather than with the functions of representation there is no need to discuss them here. There can be no doubt that it is right to emphasize that the provision of institutional arrangements for competition between politicians, including the peaceful replacement of one set of leaders by another, is an important function that a system of political representation can serve. If we were concerned with the definition of liberal democracy it might be appropriate to say that no representative system could rightly be called democratic unless it fulfilled this function. But there have been and are many political systems which are in some degree representative although they do not provide for electoral competition, and in a book on the concept of representation it is sufficient to say that this is one of the eight functions that representation can serve.

Leadership and responsibility

One of the many ways in which political activity differs from economic or social activity is that politics involves a sharp distinction between leaders and led. There are differences of power and status in economic and social activity, but almost everyone in society takes part and the personal influence that any one man or handful of men can have on the system is fairly small. Politics, on the other hand, is an activity which only a tiny minority of the population engages in on a full-time basis. All systems of government are in this sense oligarchic and a handful of political leaders can exercise immense power over their country. The selection of political leaders is a process of the utmost importance and it is a process which in many countries is performed by the representative system.

This is not the case in traditional systems of government where leaders are drawn from a ruling family or caste. Nor is it the case in military dictatorships where leaders are selected by the processes of military recruitment and promotion: which officer gets the top position in government depends on a mixture of political ambition, agility and good fortune, but there is normally a fairly small pool of senior officers from whom he emerges. But in virtually all other types of government, democratic or dictatorial, in industrialized or developing societies, politicians are normally recruited and political leaders selected through the party system. Parties interest people in politics, persuade them to accept minor offices, choose between candidates for election, groom potential leaders for stardom, and mobilize support for them when they are successful. In parliamentary systems the representative assembly plays an important part in the process because an ability to perform well in debates is a necessary requisite for ministers. In Communist systems the assembly is relatively unimportant and top leaders are normally selected from the membership of the central committee of the party. The American system is exceptional in that cabinet posts sometimes go to presidential nominees who have never held elective office or been active in party affairs, but these are temporary posts and all career politicians have to make their way up through the party system.

If one of the functions of a representative system is the selection of political leaders, another is that of giving them sufficient support and scope for them to be able to balance conflicting pressures and formulate long-term plans for their government. With elections every four or five years the horizons of politicians are inevitably limited and 'medium-term' might be a more realistic expression than 'long-term', but at least it is generally thought desirable that political leaders should accept a broader responsibility than that of responding to day-to-day pressures.

One facet of this is that it is a function of political representation not only to articulate popular demands but also to provide for their integration. As V. O. Key said: 'The problem of the politician or the statesman in a democracy is to maintain a working balance between the demands of competing interests and values. His task is not necessarily the expression of the "general will" or the "popular will".'[9]

Heinz Eulau struck a similar chord when he claimed that hetero-geneous electoral districts were functional from the point of view of the political system as a whole: 'The very circumstance of hetero-geneity in the district tends to free the representative from being readily bound by a mandate, to make for discretion and political re-sponsibility, and to enable him to integrate conflicting demands.'[10]

Another facet of the matter is the need for political leaders sometimes to take decisions which are downright unpopular. No-body wants conscription, higher taxes, credit restrictions or de-valuation, but from time to time the national interest requires such measures. The Conservative leader Lord Hailsham put this very bluntly in his speech defending the rather severe budget of 1962: 'When a government has to choose between a run on the pound and its own popularity, it has only one choice it can make. It makes it unwillingly. It must face unpopularity, loss of by-elections and even, if need be, defeat at a later general election. This is the price of responsible government.'[11]

Walter Lippmann referred to the same need when he said: 'Governments are unable to cope with reality when elected assem-blies and mass opinions become decisive in the state, when there are no statesmen to resist the inclinations of voters and there are only politicians to excite and to exploit them.'[12]

A third facet of the matter is that there occasionally arises the need for governments to undertake a major reversal of policy. The outstanding examples of recent years are President de Gaulle's decision to accept the demand of the Algerian Liberation Front for national independence and President Nixon's decision to engage in a gradual withdrawal of U.S. troops from Vietnam. To carry through policy changes of this scale requires both powers of leadership and room for manoeuvre.

It follows that the function of responsibility has certain insti-tutional implications. If responsiveness were the main function of a representative system it would be appropriate to have fre-quent elections and probably a rapid turnover of politicians. The function of public accountability implies that the turnover should not be too rapid, for unless representatives believe they have a fairly good chance of being re-elected the prospect of an election will not act as a check on their behaviour. The function of respon-sibility implies that elections should not be too frequent, for leaders need time both to carry through difficult policies and to persuade their followers that their less popular measures were justified.

This discussion of responsibility also emphasizes the value, in a modern state, of there being several levels of representation. One of the conditions of achieving both responsiveness and responsibility in government is that the raw demands made by local representatives and the spokesmen for particular interests should be transmuted by discussions within the representative system into more moderate demands which are more consonant with each other and with the interests of the nation as a whole. In this way the representative system acts not only as a set of information channels but also as a filter.

System maintenance

Rousseau opened the third chapter of *The Social Contract* with the following observation: 'The strongest is never strong enough to be always the master unless he transforms strength into right and obedience into duty.' He added that force itself does not create right and that 'we are obliged to obey only legitimate powers'.[13] The wisdom of these remarks has been confirmed time and time again, and a study of history reveals only a limited number of ways in which rulers have been able to acquire an aura of legitimacy. For many centuries in many societies heredity was the chief source of legitimacy: kings were chosen from a ruling family and it was important to be able to show an unbroken line of descent from one generation to another. In some societies it has been believed that members of a particular caste or class had an exclusive right to govern: mandarins in China, brahmins in India, the nobility in feudal Europe, the landed gentry in eighteenth-century England. In other countries, and more recently, a particular kind of training has been regarded as a qualification to govern. In military dictatorships a military training is said to confer a sense of discipline, honesty and capacity to rise above sectional interests that is lacking among civilians. In Communist countries membership of the Communist Party, with the training and understanding that goes with it, is regarded as a necessary qualification to take a leading part in administration.

In the present era of history, however, election by popular vote is the source of legitimacy that appears to command the most widespread respect. The party that wins a majority of seats in a parliamentary election is thereby given authority to govern the country for a stated number of years. In Britain even the opponents of the policy mandate theory would agree that an election victory confers a 'mandate to govern'. This mandate, which implies no more and no less than a right to govern the country in whatever way the leaders of the majority party think proper, is however conditional upon the maintenance of the rules of the game regarding the electoral system. In the Second World War the parties formed a coalition government and agreed to put off the general election that was due in 1940 until Germany was defeated, and in 1945 the prime minister asked his parliamentary colleagues to extend this electoral truce until the war with Japan was also concluded. However, the Labour leaders proved unwilling to accept this proposal and without their agreement Churchill felt he had no option but to plunge at short notice into a general election.

In the United States not even a total war is allowed to interfere with the practice of holding national elections every other year, and the American insistence that political authority should be wielded by persons who can be seen to be the people's representatives leads to the practice of electing judges, district attorneys and other officials whose European equivalents are appointed by the executive. In the Soviet Union the Stalin Constitution of 1936 established direct popular election to a considerable hierarchy of legislative bodies, with the Supreme Soviet at the top. In practice the elections are non-competitive, but great importance is attached to a large turn-out and it is clearly believed that these representative institutions, even without competition, bolster the legitimacy of the government.

The other side of the coin is that a mass boycott of elections constitutes a public refusal to re-authorize the regime which is almost certain to endanger it. A good example is the partial boycott of the Nigerian federal elections in 1964: this was successful in only 70 constituencies out of 312, but it nevertheless caused a major constitutional crisis and spelled the beginning of the end of Nigeria's experiment with representative government.

The legitimizing function of representation can also be seen where representatives are appointed rather than elected. A commission of enquiry into industrial relations would lack legitimacy in the eyes of industrial workers unless it included at least one trade unionist among its members. The microcosmic representation of the various sections of the federation in the Canadian cabinet and Supreme Court helps to bolster the legitimacy of the federal government, while the customary inclusion of a Catholic and a Jew (and now a Negro) among the nine members of the American Supreme Court does the same for that institution.

A related function of representation is the mobilization of consent. This was the original purpose of the older European parliaments, and though it would not now be said to be their main purpose it continues to be one of their more important functions. The liberal model of parliamentary government suggests that the electors control the representatives and the latter control the administrators, but on many issues the influence actually flows in the reverse direction. Problems are identified and policies framed within the administrative departments; ministers explain the proposals to their colleagues on the back benches; and the latter whip up support for the proposals by speeches in Parliament and in the country. The separation of powers prevents the process working so smoothly in the United States, which is one reason why the president has to use press conferences and public relations techniques to gain support for his policies, but there are many occasions on which speeches and campaigns by members of Congress help to persuade public opinion of the need for foreign aid, military intervention, increased taxes and other policies for which there is no spontaneous demand from the ordinary citizen.

The practice of official consultation with spokesmen for interest groups serves the same function. This is, of course, not really the intention of the interest groups, but if their negotiations with the administration are successful they are inevitably drawn into the position of agreeing (explicitly or implicitly) to persuade their members that the compromises they have arrived at are satisfactory. The general rule is that all channels of political communication tend to become two-way channels.

This rule can be seen very clearly in the operation of advisory and consultative committees. Thus, several of Britain's nationalized industries have consultative committees which were set up with the explicit purpose of representing consumers and bringing their complaints to the attention of the public corporations running the industries. In practice, close contact between the committees and the corporation officials has generally had the effect of persuading the committees that most public complaints are unjustified, and these numerous consumers' committees have on the whole been more successful in bringing the excuses and policies of the corporations to the attention of the public than in bringing public pressure to bear on the corporations. In 1970 public criticisms of the quality of British radio and television services led to the suggestion that a new Broadcasting Council should be established to oversee all the broadcasting media and deal with complaints from aggrieved members of the public. The *Daily Telegraph* made the following comment:

> Alas, this suggestion will not begin to solve the problem. It is our experience generally that boards which are set up to regulate and supervise some activity, whether on behalf of the government or the consumer, are soon captured by the industry in question and fashioned into its apologists.[14]

It is highly unlikely that this tendency is confined to Britain. The generalization that all channels of political communication become two-way channels can be supplemented by the generalization that, unless political passions are aroused, the party with most expert knowledge will tend to get the better of the argument. All representative institutions, if skilfully handled, can serve to mobilize consent to the policies of those actually running the industry, agency or government involved.

A closely related function of representation is that of relieving pressure on a regime from critics and dissenters. Representative institutions can do this partly by offering opportunities for grievances to be aired and partly by diverting the activities of potential revolutionaries into constitutional channels. Developments in British universities since 1968 provide a good example of this function. Faced with sit-ins and the prospect of other disruptive activities on the part of their students, university authorities have responded by creating new forms of representation. Student/staff committees have been established in each department and student representatives have been appointed to Senate committees and even to the Senate itself. The purpose of these moves, put bluntly, is to prevent the disruption of university life by student demonstrations and protests. The developments have other advantages, such as better communication and better understanding, but these are balanced (from the point of view of the university authorities) by the large increase in the amount of time spent on committee work. Very few people would maintain that universities run more smoothly or more effectively with student representation than they did without it in the past. The point is that they run more smoothly than they would now do without it, given the present mood among students. The object of the exercise is not to improve the decision-making process, but to moderate conflict and protect the essential features of the university system.

It is intrinsically difficult to find clear examples of disruption that did not occur, but there are ways in which the British parliamentary system serves the function of acting as a safety valve for grievances. The old slogan 'redress of grievances before supply' sums up a long chapter of parliamentary history. Questions in Parliament are an outlet for grievances and the procedure whereby normal business may be suspended for an emergency debate constitutes another safety valve. Criticisms made in the 1960s of the ease with which ministers and officials could prevent an aggrieved citizen's case being re-opened led to the creation of the post of Parliamentary Commissioner, the British equivalent of the Scandinavian *Ombudsman*. If an M.P. fails to get satisfaction at Question Time he can now refer the grievance to the commissioner, who has power to call for confidential files and demand explanations from the civil servants concerned with the case. Another new development of the 1960s, this time arising from a new social problem rather than from a procedural problem, was the establishment of the Community Relations Commission and a set of Community Councils for race relations, which take up grievances and try to remove their cause by persuasion and pressure. The local Community Relations Councils are (to some extent) representative bodies in the microcosmic sense of the term.

5

Different examples can be found in situations of political conflict and potential revolt. After the Second World War the democratic regimes of France and Italy were threatened by the existence of large and well-organized Communist parties, each able to command about four million supporters. Though Communists were largely kept out of administrative positions no attempt was made to prevent them from competing in elections, and energies that might have been spent on the barricades were devoted to canvassing and other methods of soliciting votes. The socializing effect of membership of a legislative assembly was summed up earlier in France in the often-repeated comment: 'There is more in common between two deputies only one of whom is a revolutionary than there is between two revolutionaries only one of whom is a deputy.' It is hazardous to suggest causal relationships in history, but it is the case that the Communist threat to both these regimes has been contained and relieved over the past twenty years.

In the United States some recent troubles arise partly from the fact that extremist groups have taken to the streets instead of to the ballot box. The system would clearly be more secure if the Black Panthers and their allies would concentrate on election campaigns rather than on direct action. The alienation of some student radicals is another problem, as was evidenced by the sigh of relief that was heard in 1968 when large numbers of students went canvassing for Eugene McCarthy. It can be argued that one of the needs of the American political system is to engage its radical youth in some constitutional activities connected with the representative process.

Of course, representation by election does not always prevent grievances building up. For instance, the city of Londonderry has a sizeable majority of Roman Catholics among its citizens but careful drawing of ward boundaries has led to there being a safe and permanent majority of Protestants on the City Council. The resulting resentment among Catholics, combined with other exacerbating factors, had led to intermittent riots in the city over the past fifty years, and in 1969 a particularly serious outbreak of violence led the government to suspend the City Council and hand over its functions to a new body called the Londonderry Commission. The nominated members of the commission are thought likely to represent Catholic interests more effectively than before and the move has done something to relieve pressure on the regime. A similar function has been served by the decision to transfer some of the responsibilities of Northern Irish town councils in respect of housing to a new housing authority which contains a number of members nominated to represent the Catholic community.

If representative institutions are created with the object of relieving pressure on a regime, the timing of the exercise is crucial. After the Easter Rising of 1916, it was decided to create a new body called the Irish Convention to act as a forum for discussion between representatives of all groups, including the extremists. This move was too late, the Convention failing because it was boycotted by the extremist groups whose presence was most essential. On the other hand, the Conservative Party's promise before the 1970 election to create a Scottish National Convention was clearly too early, because the Scottish Nationalists do not pose a serious threat and the establishment of such a Convention would provide them with a new platform for their demands. It is possible to draw parallels from the academic scene, since some universities have suffered from the refusal of their authorities to meet student demands until it was too late to avoid trouble while, at the other extreme, it is noticeable that the two most liberal and progressive institutions of university education in Britain have suffered more from student violence than any of the others.

In conclusion it is suggested that this analysis of the functions of political representation could serve as a general framework for empirical research. It could be used as a starting point for the classification of representative roles and relationships, while representative systems could be assessed in terms of their performance along the eight dimensions indicated. It can also serve as a basis for classifying the considerable amount of research that has been done on political representation.

8/Conclusions

The concept of representation, like those of liberty, equality and democracy, has been developed more by politicians and propagandists than by political scientists. Like these other concepts, it has favourable connotations, so that few people are openly opposed to it. Like them also, it is a rather loose concept, which has been used in different ways by different writers, each of whom tends to claim that the meaning he attributes to it is the only proper meaning. In this situation the role of the impartial scholar is to disentangle the various meanings and show their relationship to one another, just as it is his role to explain and classify the various functions which representation can serve. It may be asked, however, whether this is enough. Should the scholar leave it at that, or should he follow his analysis with an attempt at synthesis, so that the study can be concluded with a definition of the true nature and functions of representation?

My own view, very emphatically, is that he should not make any such attempt. Unlike Hanna Pitkin, I do not believe that there is any point in trying to establish that all forms of representation are essentially aspects of the same thing, which (when it is identified) can be defined as 'the real nature of representation'. I think it is clearer and more helpful to say that there are four different types of representation, which can appropriately be described as symbolic representation, delegated representation, microcosmic representation and elective representation. Equally, I do not believe that representation has any central purpose or function which can be described as 'substantive representation' or 'actual representation' and can provide a criterion for the assessment of representative institutions and processes. On the contrary, I think that representation can serve the eight functions (grouped, if one likes, into three types of function) that have been described in Chapter 7. It may be argued that some of these functions are more desirable or more important than others, but statements of this kind have to be justified in each case and cannot be said to be implied by the nature of the concept of representation.

The advantages I claim for this kind of approach are, first, that it makes for clarity; second, that it facilitates value-free analysis in a branch of the subject where many writings are value-laden; third, that it lays the theoretical foundations for generalizations (where evidence is available) about the ways in which different types of representative fulfil the various functions of representation; and fourth, that it may help in the construction of conceptual frameworks for future research. As an example of the third point, it may be helpful to mention some of the generalizations that can be made about forms of representation in relation to the function of increasing the responsiveness of the government.

Representation and responsiveness

A number of general points can be made about the probable responsiveness of different types of representative. To begin with, it can be said that delegated representatives are invariably responsive to the wishes of those they represent, for this is their function. They may enjoy some latitude in tactics but if they lose sight of the objectives of the people for whom they are acting their positions will be in jeopardy. Trade-union negotiators who agree to measures that are unacceptable to their members will normally find that their continuation as representatives is called into question. A lawyer who ignores his client's instructions is apt to find himself discharged.

While delegated representatives are more certainly responsive than other types of representative to the wishes of those they represent, are they also more likely to persuade the government of the day to be responsive? In Britain the answer to this question must be in the affirmative. It is through direct consultation with pressure-group spokesmen, more than through any other channel, that the administration acquaints itself with informed opinion. Numerous studies tell the same general story: that the government will normally go to considerable lengths to accommodate the demands of affected interests when legislation is being planned and drafted; that the government is much more resistant to changes during the parliamentary stage; but that after the legislation is on the Statute Book the department concerned is usually willing to be accommodating on questions of administration.[1]

The reasons for this, in essence, are first, that the groups have specialized information that the government probably needs, and will certainly respect; and second, that consultation with group spokesmen is the best way of ensuring the consent, or at any rate the acquiescence, of the sections of the community most directly affected by the government's policies. It is only in very exceptional circumstances that this procedure is dispensed with, as in 1970 when the government drafted its bill to reform industrial relations without consulting the trade unions, and the fact that many British unions threatened to sabotage this reform by all legal means will presumably tend to strengthen the convention that group spokesmen should normally be consulted by the government at the drafting stage.

If we turn from delegated representation to symbolic representation we turn to the other end of the spectrum, for symbolic representatives are not normally expected to respond to anyone's wishes. However, microcosmic representatives and elective representatives fall somewhere between these extremes.

That microcosmic representatives are generally expected to be more responsive than symbolic representatives is illustrated by (for instance) the complaints that immigrant groups in Britain have made about the composition of bodies dealing with race relations, it being asserted that the West Indian or Asian members of these bodies are not typical of the immigrants as a whole and are therefore no more than symbolic representatives of the immigrant communities. Critics who complain about the unrepresentative composition of the House of Commons make the further assumption that a body of elected representatives would be more likely to be responsive to popular wishes if the elected persons also represented the electorate in a microcosmic sense.

Whether these assumptions are valid is a rather difficult empirical question. It has been shown that in Britain differences of attitudes among M.P.s are to some extent related to differences of social background. In the Parliamentary Labour Party members of the older professions tend to be on the right of the party, members of newer professions such as journalism and teaching tend to be on the left, and manual workers tend to be less concerned with ideological questions and 'more concerned with the detailed implementation of social reforms'.[2] But it is not entirely clear what bearing this has on the responsiveness of (a) the Parliamentary Labour Party or (b) the House of Commons as a whole to (x) the views of constituents or (y) the views of the entire electorate. Again, it has been established that middle-class people are usually more tender-minded than working-class people,[3] and on this basis it might be argued that the over-representation of the middle classes in Parliament is responsible for the fact that in recent years Parliament has been more tender-minded than the general public on such an issue as capital punishment. But this is a rather simplistic argument and it would probably be misleading to attribute much significance to it.

In the U.S. Congress virtually all members are middle-class and about 70 per cent of them are lawyers, there having been very little change in these respects over the past century. In the light of British experience it might be suggested that this dominance by lawyers makes Congress more conservative than it would be if its members were drawn from a wider variety of occupations. But this is a highly speculative suggestion and even if it were valid it is not clear what its implications would be for the responsiveness of Congress to the views and demands of the American public. In short we do not know very much about the relationship between microcosmic representation and the responsiveness of representative bodies.

The responsiveness of elected representatives, on the other hand, has been the subject of a great deal of research. Innumerable historical studies have explained how some movements of public opinion have influenced the behaviour of elected persons and have asserted that other movements of opinion have been ignored. The election results of the past have been explained in terms of the policy issues that were debated during the campaign and it has often been said that governments (or presidents) came to power with a mandate to do various things they had promised. Since 1945 documentary studies of this kind have been supplemented by numerous sample surveys of public opinion and voting behaviour. One of the most striking conclusions to emerge from these surveys is that voters are far less concerned about policy issues than had previously been thought. Much of the American evidence on this question has been summarized by John Wahlke in an article which drew the following conclusions about the knowledge and attitudes of voters in relation to Congress:

1 Few citizens entertain interests that clearly represent 'policy demands' or 'policy expectations' or wishes and desires that are readily convertible into them.

2 Few people even have thought-out, consistent, and firmly held positions on most matters of public policy.

3 It is highly doubtful that policy demands are entertained even in the form of broad orientations, outlooks, or belief systems.

4 Large proportions of citizens lack the instrumental knowledge about political structures, processes, and actions that they would need to communicate policy demands or expectations if they had any.

5 Relatively few citizens communicate with their representatives.

6 Citizens are not especially interested or informed about the policy-making activities of their representatives as such.

7 Relatively few citizens have any clear notion that they are making policy demands or policy choices when they vote.[4]

The evidence from Britain, though not so voluminous, points in the same direction. Opinions on issues can be elicited from voters but the relationship between policy preferences and party preferences is not at all close.[5] Party preferences are to be explained partly in terms of traditional and class loyalties and partly in terms of the general image people have of the competence of the government and the opposition. The authors of one survey concluded that no more than 10 per cent of the voters in the 1951 election could have made their choice on the basis of an issue or set of issues[6] and the authors of subsequent surveys have found it impossible to isolate the issues that were important and assess their influence. Findings of this kind have destroyed the validity of the mandate theory, except as a purely normative theory about what is desirable. They have also cast doubt on some of the findings of historians: the Conservatives may have lost the 1923 election because the electors disliked the prospect of a protective tariff but it is now difficult to feel much confidence in this kind of assessment. A student of the 1950 election who used nothing but documentary sources would probably conclude that the election was dominated by the question of steel nationalization, but the polls show that the great majority of electors was totally uninterested in this issue.

However, it is possible to push this line of reasoning too far, and Miller and Stokes have indicated some important reservations. The apathy of the majority may not be crucial, they suggest, because 'the Congressman is a dealer in increments and margins' whose 'record may have a very real bearing on his electoral success or failure without most of his constituents ever knowing what that record is'.[7] Secondly, the representative may over-rate his visibility to his constituents and therefore be more responsive than he actually needs to be. Thirdly, the relationship between voters and their congressman is 'not a simple bilateral one but is complicated by the presence of all manner of intermediaries'.[8] Fourthly, the degree of popular influence varies very substantially between issues, being negligible in relation to foreign affairs but very considerable in relation to civil rights.

At the local level, the responsiveness of American city councils has been assessed in a comparative study by Prewitt and Eulau. They found that, of the 82 councils they studied, 20 were responsive to the wishes of an attentive public, 26 were responsive to ad-hoc pressure groups concerned with particular issues, and the remaining 36 'did not in any discernible manner seem to act in response to any politically organised views in the public'.[9] There was some relationship between electoral insecurity and responsiveness but lack of responsiveness did not lead to electoral discontent. What emerges from this study is not the existence of causal relationships determining the extent of responsiveness but the existence of syndromes, with one type of local political system being characterized by electoral competition, insecurity of tenure, public accountability and responsiveness while the other type of system was characterized by the opposite of all these features.

Very few direct attempts have been made to compare the responsiveness of different types of representatives dealing with similar issues and the only successful one known to the author is Peterson's study of the representation of poor people in community action programmes.[10] This study compares developments in Philadelphia, where representatives were elected by residents in poor areas of the city, New York, where representatives were chosen by community organizations in poor areas, and Chicago, where representatives were nominated by public officials. The results are conceptually as well as intrinsically interesting, particularly in the comparison between Philadelphia and New York. In the terms suggested in this book, the Philadelphia representatives can be classified as elective representatives and the New Yorkers as delegated representatives. We would expect the latter to be more certainly responsive than the former to the wishes and interests of their constituents and this expectation was fully confirmed by the study.

However, Peterson did not set it out in this way. Using Hanna Pitkin's categories of 'formal representation' and 'substantive' or 'actual representation', he regarded the methods of selection as different types of formal representation and asserted that the arrangements in New York provided for 'less formal representation' than those in Philadelphia. He then presented the result of the comparison as something of a paradox, in which the city with more formal representation ended up with less actual representation. It seems clear that this paradox is artificial and I think this example supports my view that Mrs Pitkin's categories are somewhat unhelpful (though in all fairness I must add that she is not responsible for Peterson's assumption that formal representation is something of which a group can have more or less).

A last word

It is not proposed to extend this discussion to the other functions of representation, because my object in this final chapter is simply to illustrate the advantages that I think can be gained from adopting the conceptual approach I have outlined, not to conduct anything in the nature of a general review of research. It may be appropriate, however, to end with two reflections on research in this field.

The first is that very much more research has been conducted on forms of popular control than on the other functions of representation. There have been numerous studies related to responsiveness and accountability and innumerable studies of the mechanism of peaceful change. Partly because it is easier to study elections than almost anything else and partly because of the ideological predispositions of Western political scientists, vast resources have been poured into the analysis of electoral systems, campaign methods, and voting behaviour. Not so much has been done on leadership and responsibility and very much less attention has been devoted to the role of representative institutions in system maintenance.

The second point is that the study of system maintenance has suffered more considerably than most branches of the subject from the gap between empirical and historical research. Empirical studies in this field tend to be simply in terms of public attitudes, with little or no historical perspective and without relating these attitudes to traditions, to behaviour, or to the relative efficacy of different types of institutions in mobilizing consent and support for the regime.[11] Historical studies tend to focus on unique events and not to be concerned with the illustration of general problems. It is true that the countless studies of individual revolutionary movements have recently been supplemented by comparative studies of the nature and incidence of revolution, but there is as yet no study known to the author of the ways in which representative institutions have served to precipitate, delay or avoid revolutions. It is not very original to plead for more integration between empirical and historical studies but this is an area in which the plea seems particularly relevant. For if political scientists are to gain a fuller understanding of the role of representative processes and institutions in a political system they must supplement their elaborate research into forms of popular control by systematic enquiries into the ways in which representation helps to support regimes by mobilizing consent, relieving pressure and investing the regime with an aura of legitimacy.

Notes
and
References

1/The Meaning of Representation
1 Hanna F. Pitkin, *The Concept of Representation.*
2 Ibid., pp. 10–11.
3 Ibid., p. 225.
4 Karl Marx, *Critique of Hegel's Philosophy of Right*, in T. B. Bottomore (ed.) *Karl Marx: Early Writings*, p. 58.
5 David Easton, *The Political System.*
6 In this paragraph I have changed my mind since I wrote *Representative and Responsible Government.*
7 See B. C. Parekh, 'India: A Case Study in the Ideology of Representation', mimeographed paper presented at the 7th World Congress of the International Political Science Association, Brussels, 1967.

2/Medieval Concepts and Practices
1 See Walter Ullmann, *A History of Political Thought: the Middle Ages.*
2 S. B. Chrimes, *English Constitutional History*, p. 53.
3 John Fortescue, *The Governance of England*, chap. XII.
4 Ullmann, op. cit., p. 13.
5 Ibid.
6 Ibid.
7 Christopher Hill, *Puritanism and Revolution*, p. 57.
8 Ibid., p. 58.
9 Antonio Marongiu, *Medieval Parliaments*, p. 47.
10 Ibid., p. 52.
11 Ibid., p. 62.
12 E. Perroy, cited by Marongiu, op. cit., p. 99.
13 C. H. McIlwain, 'Medieval Estates', in *Cambridge Medieval History*, p. 680.
14 Quoted ibid., p. 687.
15 Quoted in Chrimes, op. cit., p. 79. This formula remained unchanged from 1294 to 1872.
16 Helen M. Cam, *Liberties and Communities in Medieval England*, p. 225.
17 G. L. Haskins, *The Growth of English Representative Government*, p. 10.
18 William Stubbs, *Select Charters*, p. 395.
19 Cam, op. cit., pp. 226–7.

3/The Birth of Representative Government
1 A remark by John Locke quoted in J. W. N. Watkins, *Hobbes's System of Ideas*, p. 73.
2 This point is made (rather more strongly) in Pitkin, op. cit., chap. 2.

3 See John Locke, *Second Treatise of Government*, section 140.
4 For an excellent summary and criticism of Locke's political ideas see John Plamenatz, *Man and Society*, chap. 6.
5 Jean-Jacques Rousseau, *The Social Contract*, chap. XV, p. 83.
6 J. P. Kenyon, *The Stuarts*, pp. 25–7.
7 See A. S. P. Woodhouse (ed.), *Puritanism and Liberty*, p. 66.
8 Ibid., p. 56.
9 Algernon Sidney, *Discourses Concerning Government*, chap. III, p. 451.
10 *Parliamentary History*, Vol. 9, col. 421.
11 Ibid., Vol. 9, col. 435.
12 Edmund Burke, *Works*, Vol. I, p. 447.
13 Reprinted in S. K. Padover (ed.), *Thomas Jefferson on Democracy*, p. 27.
14 Ibid., p. 22.
15 See D. J. Boorstin, *The Americans: the National Experience*, pp. 489–91.
16 Ibid., p. 494.
17 See the letter quoted in Carl Becker, *The Declaration of Independence*, p. 26.
18 Alexander Hamilton *et. al.*, *The Federalist*, No. 52.
19 In a letter to S. Kercheval, quoted in Padover, op. cit., p. 35.
20 See particularly Nos. 10 and 51.
21 *The Federalist*, No. 68.
22 Isaiah Berlin, 'Montesquieu', in *Proceedings of the British Academy*, Vol. 41, Oxford University Press, London, 1956, p. 272.
23 Norman L. Torrey, *Les Philosophes*, p. 9.
24 In this paragraph I follow the convenient summary in S. E. Finer's 'Chronological Note' in the English translation of E. J. Sieyès, *What is the Third Estate?*, pp. 33–48.
25 Sieyès, op. cit., p. 58.
26 Peter Campbell, in Introduction to Sieyès, op. cit., p. 15.
27 See Giovanni Sartori, 'Representational Systems', in *International Encyclopaedia of the Social Sciences*, The Macmillan Co. and the Free Press, New York, 1968, p. 466.
28 For a succinct discussion of Robespierre's political ideas, see Alfred Cobban, *Aspects of the French Revolution*, chaps. 8 and 9.

4/Elective Representation and the Franchise

1 George Cornewall Lewis, *Remarks on the Use and Abuse of Some Politcal Terms*, p. 105.
2 Joseph Priestley, *Essay on the First Principles of Government*.
3 Richard Price, *Observations on the Nature of Civil Liberty* and *Additional Observations*.
4 See P. A. Brown, *The French Revolution in English History*, p. 84.
5 Jeremy Bentham, *Constitutional Code*, in the Bowring edition of Bentham's *Works*.
6 James Mill, *Essay on Government*, p. 84.
7 Ibid., p. 67.
8 Ibid., p. 69.
9 Ibid., p. 70.
10 Ibid., p. 73.
11 J. F. S. Ross, *Parliamentary Representation*, p. 106.
12 Ibid., p. 109.

13 Ibid., p. 112.
14 *The Times* (London), January 17, 1958.
15 In a programme called 'Let's Find Out', broadcast on September 1, 1960.
16 See H. Finer, *The British Civil Service*; H. J. Laski, *Parliamentary Government in England*; H. R. G. Greaves, *The British Constitution*; and R. K. Kelsall, *Higher Civil Servants in Britain.*
17 Clive Jenkins, 'The Labour Party and the Public Corporations', in *The Insiders*, a supplement to *Universities and the Left Review*, London, 1957, p. 31.
18 Ibid., p. 45.
19 James Mill, op. cit., p. 89.
20 Ibid., p. 90.
21 Peter Campbell, *French Electoral Systems and Elections, 1789–1957.*
22 Campbell, op. cit., gives an excellent short summary of each successive electoral system in France.
23 Quoted by J. S. Mill in *Dissertations and Discussions*, Vol. II, pp. 28–9.
24 J. S. Mill, *Considerations on Representative Government*, p. 129.
25 Ibid., p. 130.
26 The contrast between the elder and the younger Mill has been well brought out in an unpublished paper by Alan Ryan entitled 'Two Views of Democracy. James and John Stuart Mill', which was presented to the Annual Conference of the U.K. Political Studies Association in 1969.
27 J. S. Mill, *Consideration . . .*, op. cit., p. 213.
28 In this section I am greatly indebted to the concise summary in W. J. M. Mackenzie, *Free Elections.*

5/Representing Interests

 1 *The Fortnightly Review*, October 1876, p. 449.
 2 *The Nineteenth Century*, November 1877, p. 516.
 3 *The Federalist*, No. 10, p. 43. Italics added.
 4 Ibid.
 5 Ibid., p. 44.
 6 *The Federalist*, No. 52, p. 269.
 7 *The Federalist*, No. 57, pp. 292–3.
 8 Quoted in Charles O. Jones, *Every Second Year*, p. 36.
 9 *The Federalist*, No. 10, p. 47. See also No. 51, p. 266.
10 See *Nigeria: Report of the Commission appointed to enquire into the fears of Minorities and the means of allaying them*, H.M.S.O., London, Cmnd. 505 of 1958.
11 *The Federalist*, No. 51, p. 265.
12 Quoted in August O. Spain, *The Political Theory of John C. Calhoun*, p. 79.
13 John C. Calhoun, *Disquisition on Government*, p. 76.
14 Ibid., p. 14.
15 Ibid., p. 28.
16 See A. F. Bentley, *The Process of Government*, passim.
17 See David Truman, *The Governmental Process*, passim.

6/Representing Opinions

 1 See Thomas Hare, *Treatise on the Election of Representatives*, and Henry Fawcett, *Mr. Hare's Reform Bill Simplified and Explained.*

2   J. S. Mill, *Considerations on Representative Government*, p. 196.
3   Ibid., p. 201.
4   Ibid., p. 216.
5   Ibid., p. 249.
6   Ibid., pp. 209–10.
7   *Principles of Political Obligation*, Section 9.
8   A. D. Lindsay, *Essentials of Democracy*, p. 33. Italics added.
9   L. T. Hobhouse, *Liberalism*, pp. 124–5.
10 H. J. Laski and others, *The Development of the Representative System in Our Times*, p. 13.
11 Ernest Barker, *Reflections on Government*, p. 36.
12 J. Ramsay MacDonald, *Socialism and Government*, Vol. 1, p. viii.
13 Ibid., p. 21.
14 George B. Galloway, *The Legislative Process in Congress*, p. 244.
15 Walter Lippmann, *The Public Philosophy*, p. 42.
16 Charles E. Gilbert, 'Operative Doctrines of Representation', in *American Political Science Review*, Vol. 58, 1963, p. 606.
17 See Henry Maine, *Popular Government*.
18 See M. Ostrogorski, *Democracy and the Organisation of Political Parties*.
19 Sidney Low, *The Government of England*, pp. 58–9.
20 American Political Science Association, *Towards a More Responsible Two-Party System*, pp. 17–18.
21 Fritz Morstein Marx, 'Party Responsibility and the Legislative Programme', in John C. Wahlke and Heinz Eulau (eds.), *Legislative Behaviour* at p. 59.
22 Quoted in *American Political Science Review*, Vol. 57, 1963, p. 673.
23 A. H. Birch, *Representative and Responsible Government*, p. 121.
24 Heinz Eulau, 'Changing Views of Representation', reprinted in *Micro-Macro Political Analysis*, p. 77.
25 Ibid.
26 Ibid., p. 83.
27 Quoted in 'Political and Economic Planning', *Advisory Committees in British Government*, p. 6.

7/The Functions of Representation

1   David E. Apter, *Some Conceptual Approaches to the Study of Modernisation*, p. 311.
2   Henry B. Mayo, *An Introduction to Democratic Theory*, p. 60.
3   John C. Wahlke, Heinz Eulau, William Buchanan and Leroy C. Ferguson, *The Legislative System*, pp. 270–2.
4   Ibid., p. 394.
5   Ibid., p. 274.
6   J. Roland Pennock, 'Political Representation: an Overview', in J. Roland Pennock and John W. Chapman (eds), *Representation*, p. 13.
7   Joseph A. Schumpeter, *Capitalism, Socialism and Democracy*, p. 269.
8   Quoted in Mayo, op. cit., p. 97.
9   V. O. Key, *Politics, Parties and Pressure Groups*, p. 10.
10 Heinz Eulau, *Micro-Macro Political Analysis*, p. 205.
11 *House of Lords Debates*, April 23, 1962.
12 Walter Lippmann, *The Public Philosophy*, p. 46.
13 Rousseau, *The Social Contract*, pp. 8–9.
14 *Daily Telegraph*, January 4, 1971.

8/Conclusions

1 The best general studies of pressure group activities in Britain are S. E. Finer, *Anonymous Empire*, and Allen M. Potter, *Organised Groups in British National Politics*.

2 J. Blondel, *Voters, Parties and Leaders*, p. 147.

3 See H. J. Eysenck, *The Psychology of Politics*.

4 John Wahlke, 'Public Policy and Representative Government: the Role of the Represented', mimeographed paper prepared for the 7th World Congress of the International Political Science Association, 1967.

5 See Blondel, op. cit., pp. 75–87.

6 R. S. Milne and H. C. Mackenzie, *Straight Fight*, p. 139.

7 Warren E. Miller and Donald E. Stoke , 'Constituency Influence in Congress', in *American Political Science Review*, Vol. 57, 1963, p. 55.

8 Ibid.

9 Kenneth Prewitt and Heinz Eulau, 'Political Matrix and Political Representation', in *American Political Science Review*, Vol. 63, 1969, p. 429.

10 Paul E. Peterson, 'Forms of Representation: Participation of the Poor in the Community Action Program', in *American Political Science Review*, Vol. 64, 1970.

11 Some examples are Gabriel Almond and Sidney Verba, *The Civic Culture*, Ian Budge, *Agreement and the Stability of Democracy*, and J. Dennis, L. Lindberg and D. McCrone, 'Support for Nation and Government among English Children', in *British Journal of Political Science*, Vol. 1 1971.

Bibliography

The handful of texts on representation which have acquired the status of classics have all been discussed in this book and need not be singled out for special mention here. In addition to these, there is a large literature of theoretical and propagandist works in favour of this or that view of the proper nature of representation; an even larger literature on the working of representative institutions; and an ever-growing number of studies of the political behaviour of both represented and representatives. It would not be feasible to list all these works and it is not easy to draw a clear line between those which raise problems of conceptual interest and those which do not. Accordingly, this bibliography is restricted to (a) the books to which I have referred in the text and (b) a limited number of other books which seem to me to be of central importance.

ALMOND, GABRIEL and VERBA, SIDNEY, *The Civic Culture*, Little, Brown & Co., Boston 1965.

AMERICAN POLITICAL SCIENCE ASSOCIATION, *Towards a More Responsible Two-Party System*, Rinehart & Co., New York 1950.

APTER, DAVID E., *Some Conceptual Approaches to the Study of Modernisation*, Prentice-Hall, Englewood Cliffs, N.J. 1968.

BACHRACH, PETER, *The Theory of Democratic Elitism*, Little, Brown & Co., Boston 1967.

BARKER, ERNEST, *Reflections on Government*, Oxford University Press, London 1942.

BECKER, CARL L., *The Declaration of Independence*, Harcourt Brace & Co., New York 1922, reprinted 1942.

BEER, SAMUEL H., *Modern British Politics*, Faber & Faber, London 1965.

BENTHAM, JEREMY, *Collected Works* (ed. John Bowring), William Tait, Edinburgh 1843.

BENTLEY, A. F., *The Process of Government*, first published 1908, second edition Principia Press, Bloomington, Indiana 1935.

BERELSON, BERNARD, LAZARSFELD, PAUL and McPHEE, WILLIAM, *Voting*, Chicago University Press, Chicago 1954.

BIRCH, A. H., *Representative and Responsible Government*, Allen & Unwin, London 1964.

——— *Small-Town Politics*, Oxford University Press, London 1959.

BLONDEL, JEAN, *Voters, Parties and Leaders*, Penguin Books, Harmondsworth, Middlesex 1963.

BOORSTIN, DANIEL J., *The Americans: the National Experience*, Penguin Books, Harmondsworth, Middlesex 1969.

BOTTOMORE, T. B., *Elites and Society*, Watts, London 1964.

——— (ed.), *Karl Marx: Early Writings*, McGraw-Hill, New York 1964.

BROWN, P. A., *The French Revolution in English History*, Lockwood & Sons, London 1918.

BUDGE, IAN, *Agreement and the Stability of Democracy*, Markham Publishing Co., Chicago 1970.

BURKE, EDMUND, *Works*, Bohn's Standard Library, London 1887.

BURNS, JAMES M., *The Deadlock of Democracy*, John Calder, London 1964.

BUTLER, DAVID and ROSE, RICHARD, *The British General Election of 1959*, Macmillan, London 1960.

BUTLER, DAVID and STOKES, DONALD, *Political Change in Britain*, Macmillan, London 1969.

BUTLER, J. R. M., *The Passing of the Great Reform Bill*, Longmans, London 1914.

CALHOUN, JOHN C., *Disquisition on Government*, first published in 1853, reprinted by Peter Smith, New York 1943.

CAM, HELEN M., *Liberties and Communities in Medieval England*, Cambridge University Press, Cambridge 1944 and Merlin Press, London 1963.

CAMPBELL, ANGUS, CONVERSE, PHILIP E., MILLER, WARREN and STOKES, DONALD E., *The American Voter*, John Wiley & Sons, New York 1960.

CAMPBELL, PETER, *French Electoral Systems and Elections, 1789–1957*, Faber & Faber, London 1958.

CHRIMES, S. B., *English Constitutional History*, Oxford University Press, London 1947, fourth edition 1967.

COBBAN, ALFRED, *Aspects of the French Revolution*, Paladin, London 1971.

DAHL, ROBERT A., *A Preface to Democratic Theory*, Chicago University Press, Chicago 1956.

DE GRAZIA, ALFRED, *Public and Republic*, A. A. Knopf, New York 1951.

EASTON, DAVID, *The Political System*, A. A. Knopf, New York 1953.

EULAU, HEINZ, *Micro-Macro Political Analysis*, Aldine Publishing Co., Chicago 1969.

EULAU, HEINZ, ELDERSVELD, SAMUEL J. and JANOWITZ, MORRIS, *Political Behaviour*, The Free Press, Glencoe, Illinois 1956.

EYSENCK, H. J., *The Psychology of Politics*, Routledge & Kegan Paul, London 1954.

FARRAND, MAX, *The Framing of the Constitution of the United States*, Yale University Press, New Haven 1913.

—— *The Records of the Federal Convention of 1787*, 4 vols., Yale University Press, New Haven 1911.

FAWCETT, H., *Mr. Hare's Reform Bill Simplified and Explained*, T. Brettell, London 1860.

FINER, HERMAN, *The British Civil Service*, Allen & Unwin, London 1937.

FINER, S. E., *Anonymous Empire*, The Pall Mall Press, London 1958.

—— *Comparative Government*, Allen Lane The Penguin Press, London 1970.

FORTESCUE, SIR JOHN, *The Governance of England*, written 1471, first printed edition 1546, revised edition, ed. Charles Plummer, The Clarendon Press, Oxford 1885.

FRIEDRICH, CARL J., *Constitutional Government and Democracy*, Ginn & Co., Boston 1950.

GALLOWAY, G. B., *The Legislative Process in Congress*, Thomas Crowell, New York 1953.

GIBBONS, P. A., *Ideas of Political Representation in Parliament*, Basil Blackwell, Oxford 1914.

GOOCH, G. P., *English Democratic Ideas in the Seventeenth Century*, Cambridge University Press, Cambridge 1954.

Greaves, H. R. G., *The British Constitution*, Allen & Unwin, London 1938.

GREEN, T. H., *Principles of Political Obligation*, first published 1882, new edition Longmans, Green & Co., London 1941.

HAMBURGER, Joseph, *Intellectuals in Politics: John Stuart Mill and the Philosophic Radicals*, Yale University Press, New Haven, 1965.

HAMILTON, ALEXANDER, JAY, JOHN and MADISON, JAMES, *The Federalist*, first published 1787-8, new edition Everyman's Library, London 1918

HANSON, ROYCE, *The Political Thicket: Reapportionment and Constitutional Democracy*, Prentice-Hall, Englewood Cliffs, N.J. 1966.

HARE, THOMAS, *A Treatise on the Election of Representatives*, Longman, Brown, Green, Longmans, and Roberts, London 1859.

HASKINS, GEORGE L., *The Growth of English Representative Government*, Oxford University Press, London 1948.

H.M.S.O., *Nigeria: Report of the Commission appointed to enquire into the fears of Minorities and the means of allaying them*, London, Cmnd. 505 of 1958.

HILL, CHRISTOPHER, *Puritanism and Revolution*, Secker and Warburg, London 1958.

HOBBES, THOMAS, *Leviathan*, first published 1651, new edition ed. Michael Oakeshott, Basil Blackwell, Oxford 1946.

HOBHOUSE, L. T., *Liberalism*, first published 1911, reprinted Thornton Butterworth, London 1934.

HOFSTADTER, RICHARD, *The American Political Tradition and the Men Who Made It*, Vintage Books, New York 1945.

JEFFERSON, THOMAS, *The Life and Selected Writings of Jefferson*, ed. A. Koch and W. Peden, The Modern Library, New York 1944.

—— *Thomas Jefferson on Democracy*, ed. S. K. Padover, Mentor Books, New York 1946.

JONES, Charles O., *Every Second Year*, The Brookings Institution, Washington 1967.

KELSALL, R. K., *Higher Civil Servants in Britain*, Routledge & Kegan Paul, London 1955.

KENDALL, WILLMOORE, *John Locke and the Doctrine of Majority Rule*, Illinois University Press, Urbana, Illinois 1941.

KENYON, J. P., *The Stuarts*, Collins Fontana Library, London 1966.

KEY, V. O., *Politics, Parties and Pressure Groups*, Crowell, New York (third edition) 1952.

—— *Public Opinion and American Democracy*, A. A. Knopf, New York 1961.

LASKI, H. J., *Parliamentary Government in England*, Allen & Unwin, London 1938.

LASKI, H. J. *et al.*, *The Development of the Representative System in Our Times*, Geneva 1928.

LEWIS, GEORGE CORNEWALL, *Remarks on the Use and Abuse of Some Political Terms*, first published 1832, new edition James Thornton, Oxford 1877.

LINDSAY, A. D., *The Essentials of Democracy*, Oxford University Press, (second edition), London 1935.

LIPPMANN, WALTER, *The Public Philosophy*, Little, Brown, Boston 1955.

LOCKE, JOHN, *Two Treatises of Government*, first published 1690, new edition ed. Peter Laslett, Cambridge University Press, Cambridge 1960.

LOW, SIDNEY J., *The Governance of England*, T. Fisher Unwin, London 1904.

MACDONALD, JAMES RAMSAY, *Socialism and Government*, Independent Labour Party, London 1909.

MCILWAIN, C. H. (ed.), *Cambridge Medieval History*, Cambridge University Press, Cambridge 1932.

MACKENZIE, W. J. M., *Free Elections*, Allen & Unwin, London 1958.
MCKENZIE, R. T., *British Political Parties*, Wm. Heinemann, London 1955.
MADISON, JAMES, *The Forging of American Federalism*, selected writings ed. S. K. Padover, Harper & Row, New York 1965.
MAINE, SIR HENRY, *Popular Government*, John Murray, London 1886.
MARONGUI, ANTONIO, *Medieval Parliaments*, Eyre & Spottiswood, London 1968.
MAYO, HENRY B., *An Introduction to Democratic Theory*, Oxford University Press, New York 1960.
MILL, JAMES, *Essay on Government*, first published 1828, reprinted Bobbs-Merrill, New York 1955.
MILL, JOHN STUART, *Autobiography*, first published 1873, new edition, Oxford University Press, London 1924.
——— *Considerations on Representative Government*, first published 1861, new edition ed. R. B. McCallum, Basil Blackwell, Oxford 1946.
——— *Dissertations and Discussions*, Longmans, London 1859.
MILNE, R. S. and MACKENZIE, H. C., *Straight Fight*, Hansard Society, London 1954.
MONTESQUIEU, BARON, *The Spirit of the Laws*, first published 1748, new edition ed. F. Neumann, Hafner Classics, New York 1969.
OSTROGORSKI, M., *Democracy and the Organisaion of Political Parties*, Macmillan, London 1902.
PENNOCK, J. ROLAND and CHAPMAN, JOHN W. (eds.), *Representation*, Atherton Press, New York 1968.
PITKIN, HANNA F., *The Concept of Representation*, California University Press, Berkeley and Los Angeles 1967.
PLAMENATZ, JOHN, *Man & Society*, Longmans, Green, London 1963.
POLITICAL AND ECONOMIC PLANNING, *Advisory Committees in British Government*, Allen and Unwin, London 1960.
POLSBY, NELSON W., *Community Power and Political Theory*, Yale University Press, New Haven 1963.
POTTER, ALLEN M., *Organised Groups in British National Politics*, Faber & Faber, London 1961.
PRICE, RICHARD, *Additional Observations on the Value of Civil Liberty*, T. Cadell, London 1777.
——— *Observations on the Nature of Civil Liberty*, T. Cadell, London 1776.
PRIESTLEY, JOSEPH, *An Essay on the First Principles of Government*, J. Johnson, London 1768.
RAE, DOUGLAS W., *The Political Consequences of Electoral Laws*, Yale University Press, New Haven 1967.
ROSS, J. F. S., *Parliamentary Representation*, Eyre & Spottiswood, London 1948.
ROUSSEAU, JEAN-JACQUES, *The Social Contract*, first published 1762, new edition, Everyman's Library, London 1913.
SCHATTSCHNEIDER, E. E., *The Semisovereign People*, Holt, Rinehart & Winston, New York 1960.
SCHUMPETER, J. A., *Capitalism, Socialism and Democracy*, Harper Bros., New York 1942.
SIDNEY, ALGERNON, *Discourses Concerning Government*, London 1698.
SIEYES, E. J., *What is the Third Estate?*, first published Paris 1789, English translation ed. S. E. Finer, Pall Mall Press, London 1963.
SPAIN, A. O., *The Political Theory of John C. Calhoun*, Brookman Associates, New York 1951.

STUBBS, WILLIAM, *Select Charters and other Illustrations of English Constitutional History*, ninth edition, The Clarendon Press, Oxford 1929.

TOCQUEVILLE, ALEXIS DE, *Democracy in America*, first published 1862, new edition ed. J. P. Mayer and Max Lerner, Harper & Row, New York 1966.

TORREY, N. L., *Les Philosophes*, Capricorn Books, New York 1960.

TRUMAN, DAVID B., *The Governmental Process*, A. A. Knopf, New York 1951.

ULLMANN, WALTER, *A History of Political Thought: The Middle Ages*, Penguin Books, Harmondsworth, Middlesex 1965.

WAHLKE, JOHN C. and EULAU, HEINZ (eds.), *Legislative Behaviour*, The Free Press, Glencoe, Illinois 1959.

WAHLKE, JOHN C., EULAU, HEINZ, BUCHANAN, WILLIAM and FERGUSON, LEROY C., *The Legislative System*, John Wiley & Sons, New York 1962.

WATKINS, J. W. N., *Hobbes's System of Ideas*, Hutchinson, London 1965.

WILLIAMS, PHILIP M., *Crisis and Compromise: Politics in the Fourth Republic*, Longmans, London 1964.

WOODHOUSE, A. S. P. (ed.), *Puritanism and Liberty*, J. M. Dent & Sons, London 1951.

WOODWARD, E. L., *French Revolutions*, Oxford University Press, London, 1934.

Index